Are Environmental Regulations Driving U.S. Industry Overseas?

The Conservation Foundation is a nonprofit research and communications organization dedicated to encouraging human conduct to sustain and enrich life on earth. Since its founding in 1948, it has attempted to provide intellectual leadership in the cause of wise management of the earth's resources.

Are Environmental Regulations Driving U.S. Industry Overseas?

by H. Jeffrey Leonard

The Conservation Foundation
Washington, D.C.

Are Environmental Regulations Driving U.S. Industry Overseas?
© 1984 by The Conservation Foundation. All rights reserved. No part of this book may be reproduced in any form without the permission of The Conservation Foundation.

Typography by Rings-Leighton, Ltd., Washington, D.C.
Printed by Wickersham Printing Company, Inc., Lancaster, Pennsylvania

The Conservation Foundation
1717 Massachusetts Avenue, N.W.
Washington, D.C. 20036

Library of Congress Cataloging in Publication Data
Leonard, H. Jeffrey.
    Are environmental regulations driving U.S. industry overseas?
    Includes bibliographies and index.
    1. Industry—Location. 2. International business enterprises—Location. 3. Environmental policy—Economic aspects—United States. I. Title.

HC79.D5L45   1984   338.6'042'0973   84-17603

ISBN 0-89164-080-0

Contents

Foreword *by William K. Reilly*   ix

Preface   xiii

Executive Summary   xvii

1. Fears of an Industrial Exodus   1

  The Industrial-Flight Hypothesis   2
    Pollution-Control Costs   2
    Blockage of Plant Construction and Expansion   3
    Constraints on Hazardous Production   4
  Reactions to the Prospects of Relocation   6
    The Politics of "Flight"   6
    Government's Responses   7
  A Need for Data   9
  References   10

2. Foreign Investments and U.S. Imports by High-Pollution
    Industries   15

  Industrial Sectors Most Susceptible to Relocation   17
  Foreign Investment and Import Trends   21
    High-Pollution Industries Compared with All U.S.
      Manufacturing Industries   22
        Investments   22
        Annual Capital Expenditures   22
        U.S. Imports   25
    Investments in, and Trade with, Less-Developed
      Countries   28
        Investments   30
        Annual Capital Expenditures   31
        U.S Imports   33
  Conclusions   33
  References   36

3. Mineral-Processing Industries   41

  Metal Processors   42
    Copper   44
    Zinc   51
    Lead   55
    Arsenic Trioxide   59
  Nonmetallic-Mineral Producers   63

Asbestos 63
Cement 70
Conclusions 75
References 76

4. Chemical Industries 83

Inorganic Chemicals 83
Hydrofluoric Acid 86
Titanium Dioxide 90
Organic Chemicals 94
Primary Organic Chemicals 97
Furfural 99
Carbon Black 103
Intermediate Organic Chemicals 105
Finished Organic Chemical Products 112
Benzidine-Based Dyes 113
Pesticides 117
Conclusions 123
References 123

5. Planning for the Future 131

Industry-by-Industry Effects of Environmental
Regulations 131
High Growth Industries Not Pushed Overseas 132
A Few Industries Affected 133
Environmental Regulation as a Cocatalyst 133
Environmental Regulation as a Primary
Location Factor 134
Characteristics of Affected Industries 134
Policy Implications 137
General Trends 137
Declining Hazardous Industries 137
Mineral Processing 139
Intermediate Chemicals 139
An Integrative Approach 140

Index 141

Figures

2. FOREIGN INVESTMENTS AND U.S. IMPORTS BY
HIGH-POLLUTION INDUSTRIES

2.1   Plant and Equipment Expenditures for Pollution
Control, 1973-1982   18

2.2   Percentage of All Manufacturing-Industry Plant
and Equipment Expenditures for Pollution
Control Made by Four High-Pollution Sectors,
1973-1982   19

2.3   Pollution-Control Expenditures as Percentage of
Plant and Equipment Expenditures, 1973-1982   20

2.4   Foreign Direct Investment by U.S. Companies,
1971-1981   23

2.5   Percentage of Foreign Direct Investment by U.S.
Marketing Industries Occupied by Chemical and
Mineral-Processing Sectors, 1973-1980   23

2.6   Annual Capital Expenditures by Majority-Owned
Foreign Affiliates of U.S. Companies, 1971-1983   24

2.7   Percentage of High-Pollution-Sector
Manufacturing in Annual Capital Expenditures by
Majority-Owned Foreign Affiliates of U.S.
Companies, 1971-1983   26

2.8   U.S. Imports of All Manufactured Goods and of
Chemicals, Processed Minerals, and Pulp and
Paper, 1971-1981   27

2.9   Percentage of Chemicals, Processed Minerals, and
Pulp and Paper in Total U.S. Imports of
Manufactured Goods, 1971-1981   28

2.10   Exports to the United States by Majority-Owned
Foreign Affiliates of U.S. Companies, 1966-1976   29

2.11   Percentage of Chemicals and Processed Minerals
in Total Manufactured Goods Exported to the
United States by Majority-Owned Foreign
Affiliates of U.S. Companies, 1966-1976   30

2.12 Percentage of U.S. Foreign Direct Investment
      Located in Less-Developed Countries, 1970-1980   31

2.13 Percentage of Annual Overseas Capital
      Expenditures by U.S. Affiliates Going to Less-
      Developed Countries, 1971-1983   32

2.14 Percentage of U.S. Imports Coming from Less-
      Developed Countries, 1972-1981   34

3. MINERAL-PROCESSING INDUSTRIES

3.1 U.S. Imports and Exports of Copper, 1975-1982   46

3.2 U.S. Productive Capacity, Production, and
     Imports of Slab Zinc, 1970-1982   52

3.3 U.S. Production, Imports, and Exports of
     Primary Refined Lead, 1973-1982   57

3.4 World Production, U.S. Production, and U.S.
     Imports of Arsenic Trioxide, 1968-1982   61

3.5 U.S. Imports of Asbestos Yarns, Silvers, etc., by
     Country of Origin, 1972-1982   68

3.6 U.S. Imports of Asbestos Pipes, Tubes, and Fit-
     tings, by Country of Origin, 1972-1982   69

3.7 U.S. Imports of Cement and Clinker, 1970-1981   72

4. CHEMICAL INDUSTRIES

4.1 U.S. Production and Imports of Hydrofluoric
     Acid, 1970-1981   88

4.2 U.S. Production and Imports of Titanium
     Dioxide, 1970-1982   91

4.3 U.S. Imports of Furfural, 1965-1982   101

4.4 U.S. Imports of Carbon Black, 1972-1982   106

4.5 U.S. Imports of Butadiene, 1972-1982   108

4.6 U.S. Imports of Thiourea, Thiourea Dioxide, and
     Related Derivatives, 1972-1979   110

4.7 U.S. Imports of Benzenoid Intermediates and
     Finished Benzenoid Products, 1973-1982   111

4.8 U.S. Imports of Direct Dyes, 1973-1982   116

4.9 U.S. Imports of Benzenoid Pesticides, 1973-1982   119

Foreword

Are federal environmental laws impeding needed industrial development, diverting capital from productive investments, and costing the economy much-needed jobs in key industries? Heated debate over such questions has taken place within the Reagan administration, in Congress, in corporate boardrooms, in public forums, and, indeed, among environmentalists in recent years.

The debate about the cumulative economic impacts of the nation's environmental laws has moved beyond the question of direct influence on macroeconomic indicators—gross national product, rate of inflation, unemployment. Most observers now agree that the price for a cleaner environment has been marginal, according to these measures (though the costs to specific companies and some industries has been considerable).

Of greater concern is the more elusive question of the possible long-term impacts of environmental regulations on America's industrial future. In particular, some fear that the labyrinth of regulations drives industrial facilities out of business and firms out of the country, as well as hinders the construction of new plants within the United States at a time when renewed industrial growth is a national priority.

Such concerns cannot be taken lightly. Some observers suggest that in deference to future industrial expansion, environmental regulations should be reexamined and that some of those regulations should be temporarily postponed, overridden (as in the highly touted proposal to create an Energy Mobilization Board), rewritten, or canceled. At the same time, the last four years have underscored the fact that neither Congress nor the U.S. public is prepared to initiate a sweeping rollback of environmental regulations without convincing evidence that they are indeed hobbling new industrial growth.

Since 1979, The Conservation Foundation has sought to examine whether environmental regulations are driving more industries to construct plants overseas and, in effect, to export jobs rather than manufactured goods. Evidence of detrimental impacts has been largely anecdotal. Reports have circulated occasionally that particular companies are fleeing U.S. regulations to foreign "pollution havens" where expenditures can be minimized. Some companies have threatened that they will be forced to leave unless U.S. regulations are relaxed.

In the mid-1970s, environmental regulations, coupled with local public activism, were blamed by company officials for the cancellation of several large oil refineries in the East, the SOHIO pipeline in southern California, a proposed BASF chemical plant in South Carolina, and Dow Chemical's proposed plant in northern California, among others.

This report presents the results of the Foundation's efforts to determine whether the reported instances of "industrial flight" and blocked plant construction have been indicators of significant trends or exceptions to the rule. Emphasis is placed on the handful of large industries responsible for over two-thirds of all pollution-control expenditures in recent years—petroleum refining, chemicals, mineral processing, and pulp and paper.

In general, the Foundation has uncovered no evidence in overall statistics on foreign investments by U.S. companies and on U.S. imports of manufactured goods that key high-pollution industries have shifted more production facilities overseas in response to environmental regulations. Yet this study does show that, in a few high-pollution, hazardous-production industries, environmental regulations and workplace-health standards have become a more prominent and possibly decisive factor in industrial location and have led U.S. firms to move production abroad.

Examples of such industries are those that produce highly toxic, dangerous, or carcinogenic products, such as asbestos, benzidine dyes, and a few pesticides. Environmental regulations appear to have played a less decisive but still contributing role in causing basic mineral-processing industries such as copper, zinc, and lead to expand activities abroad. For these latter industries, environmental regulations have combined with other changing locational incentives and economic problems to speed international dispersion.

Nevertheless, this heavily documented study concludes that growing U.S. industries have not been forced overseas by either environmental regulations or public concern about environmental problems in the United States. Thus, the case-by-case examples of industrial flight do not appear to portend any significant adverse effects of environmental regulations on the U.S. economy in the future.

This Issue Report is the fourth major study released under the Foundation's Industrial Siting Project. Previously published were two books by Christopher J. Duerksen, the project's principal investigator:

Dow vs. California: A Turning Point in the Envirobusiness Struggle and *Environmental Regulation of Industrial Plant Siting: How to Make It Work Better.* Dr. Robert G. Healy, staff economist, authored an Issue Report, *America's Industrial Future: An Environmental Perspective.* In addition, project staff have published numerous articles in law, economics, business, and political science journals. A final report on environmental regulations and industrial location in rapidly industrializing nations, based on case studies in four nations and conducted by Mr. Leonard, will be published by the Foundation in late 1984.

The Foundation's Industrial Siting Project has been generously supported by The German Marshall Fund of the United States, The Ford Foundation, and the Richard King Mellon Foundation. Supplemental support for several additional activities undertaken in the research for this report was provided by the Foundation's donors of unrestricted support, the Princeton Committee for West European Studies, and the Center for the Study of World Politics.

William K. Reilly
President
The Conservation Foundation

Preface

This study attempts to evaluate whether U.S. environmental and workplace-health regulations have induced U.S. manufacturing industries to construct more facilities overseas and to import a larger share of goods intended for consumption in the United States. It is part of a larger project undertaken by The Conservation Foundation to determine how the advent of stringent environmental regulations in the United States and other developed countries has affected worldwide industrial-location trends.

The Foundation's inquiries into this subject have been guided by two separate but related theories that became prominent in the late 1970s and predicted how environmental regulations would affect the international industrial-siting picture. The first was that regulation would increasingly push industries out of the United States and other advanced industrial nations (the industrial-flight hypothesis); the second was that less-developed countries would compete to attract multinational industries by purposely not enacting their own pollution regulations (the pollution-haven hypothesis). The combination of the push out of industrial countries and the pull toward less-industrialized countries was expected to exert a powerful influence on international-location patterns and, as well, to enhance national strategies for industrial development in the Third World.

The focus of this book is on the industrial-flight hypothesis and whether it is applicable to the United States. The study analyzes recent foreign investment and import trends by U.S. firms to determine whether pollution-control and workplace-health standards have pushed U.S. industries abroad and whether the U.S. industrial base and balance of trade have been negatively affected.

I have written a companion report, to be published separately by The Conservation Foundation, which evaluates the pollution-haven hypothesis by exploring whether certain rapidly industrializing countries have intentionally styled themselves as pollution havens to enhance their industrial-development efforts and whether U.S. companies have sought to take advantage of such opportunities. That report, *Pollution and Multinational Corporations in Rapidly Industrializing Countries,* draws on case-study research that I conducted in four countries—Ireland, Spain, Romania, and Mexico. In the process, the economic, political, and public-health dangers for governments of underindustrialized countries following a pollution-haven strategy are illustrated, as well as the problems encountered by multinational companies that have blithely assumed that underindustrialized countries have too many more-important concerns to take punitive action in relation to pollution.

A word about the methodology pursued in research and writing this report, *Are Environmental Regulations Driving U.S. Industry Overseas?*, is in order. To test for evidence of the validity of the industrial-flight hypothesis, two types of information are necessary: statistical data that identify changes in overseas investment patterns and international trade patterns of U.S. industries; and information that sheds light on the reasons for the statistical trends and the motivations of the crucial actors responsible—U.S. companies that operate manufacturing facilities abroad and that trade raw materials and finished products in international markets. Without knowledge of the internal conditions that affect the companies in so-called pollution-intensive industries, the aggregate data can invalidate the hypothesis only by failing to conform to expected trends.

As it is, the data do help to eliminate some possibilities from further consideration but do not invalidate the hypothesis altogether. Thus, the methodological approach followed in this study is one of winnowing down to particular problem areas by establishing a series of tests whose results set the terms for the next level of inquiry. It is analogous to peeling away the layers of an onion to reveal, ultimately, the core of the problem.

First, it is necessary to identify industries that have encountered extreme difficulties as a result of environmental regulations and concern about environmental problems. To do so, capital spending on pollution controls in the last decade is examined for all U.S. industries and for key industrial sectors. In addition, several other indicators of environmental difficulties for industry are examined as a cross-check in selecting the industries most susceptible to industrial flight.

Second, some means of assessing whether trade and investment patterns follow the expectations of the hypothesis must be devised. To do this, aggregate figures for foreign investment and imports by key U.S. industrial sectors identified as pollution-intensive are examined. If overseas investments and imports by these industries have increased rapidly in recent years, and if a growing share of this activity involves countries outside of the other heavily industrialized nations, it is possible to conclude, at a minimum, that recent trends conform to those expected.

However, the trade and investment statistics alone cannot provide the crucial information necessary to know whether the environmental factors have caused the trends, have influenced them, or have only been incidental. Thus, individual industries that show large increases in foreign investments and U.S. imports are analyzed within the whole range of political-economic factors that have affected them in recent years. This requires recourse to numerous industry reports, knowledge of the impacts of particular regulations, and a general analysis of industry trade and economic factors.

I am extremely grateful to all of my colleagues from The Conservation Foundation who have contributed to this book. Debbie Johnson and Anthony Brown figured most prominently in the preparation of the many drafts that this manuscript experienced. Christopher Duerksen, Jack Noble, Robert Healy, Terry Davies, and Frances Irwin read some or all of the chapters and made extensive suggestions that I have attempted to incorporate into this final version. Bradley Rymph, following in the tradition of Foundation editors, got involved much more substantively than editors usually do, providing valuable suggestions for editorial and organizational changes that greatly streamlined this manuscript.

H. Jeffrey Leonard
August 1984

Executive Summary

During the 1970s, many U.S. observers expressed concern that the costs of complying with environmental regulations might be emerging as a significant factor in the competitiveness and location of industries involved in world trade. Although each group proposed different remedies, policy makers, labor unions, business leaders, environmentalists, and academics all predicted that strict domestic pollution-control standards might adversely affect U.S. industry's ability to compete domestically with imported products, as well as in foreign markets. They expected that, as one response, U.S. firms—particularly multinational corporations with experience operating overseas—would shift more production facilities to countries where regulatory costs could be reduced.

This prospect encouraged debate within the United States about such a shift's possible long-term effects on domestic employment, the balance of trade, the U.S. industrial base, and national security. Industry leaders frequently charged that environmental regulations were constraining, or actually reducing, overall U.S. productive capacity and thereby pushing U.S. firms to locate abroad. Others worried about the international implications, arguing that U.S. companies should abide by universal environmental standards even in countries that were willing to become "pollution havens" to attract foreign investment and industrial development.

These debates have intensified during recent years as a result of several factors: Low output and high unemployment continue in many large industries that have been hit with high regulatory costs. Industry and now the Reagan administration have increased their efforts to water down or restructure government environmental regulations (for example, by revising the Clean Air Act or exempting specific industries from certain regulations). There is a growing emphasis on stimulating U.S. exports, and "reindustrialization" of the United States itself is being proposed as a national priority.

Since 1979, The Conservation Foundation has monitored key U.S. industries to assess whether, in fact, there is any indication that environmental regulations actually have pushed large numbers of U.S.-based industries abroad and have thereby negatively affected the U.S. industrial base. Three crucial conclusions are apparent from the research:

I. *Environmental regulations have not caused a significant exodus of U.S. industries.* An investigation of recent overseas investment and foreign trade patterns by U.S. manufacturing industries from 1970 to 1982 shows that:

- No large-scale movement abroad by U.S.-based industries has occurred; nor, despite the enactment of numerous environmental laws, have the overall overseas investment patterns of U.S. industries changed significantly during the past decade.
- Although environmental regulations have had major economic impacts on U.S.-based industries, regulatory burdens usually have not been substantial enough to offset the advantages of producing in the United States. In other words, regulatory costs have not overridden more traditional factors—market considerations, transportation and labor costs, political stability—that determine how most firms select overseas locations for branch-plant construction.
- In fact, even the data for the industrial sectors that have borne the vast majority of all pollution-control expenditures in the United States—mineral processing, chemicals (including petrochemicals), and pulp and paper—do not show large increases in total overseas investment, large shifts to developing countries, or large jumps in U.S. imports of "pollution-intensive" goods.
- However, there are some indications in the overall data on foreign investments and imports that a few particular industries within the mineral-processing and chemical sectors may have responded to more stringent environmental regulations in the United States by moving more production facilities abroad. Such a finding prompted The Conservation Foundation to undertake extensive investigations of specific industries within these two pollution-prone sectors.

II. *According to The Conservation Foundation's industry-by-industry studies, a few troubled industries producing certain types of chemicals and processed minerals have been more susceptible than most to relocation pressures as a result of environmental regulations.* Those identified in this report tend to fall into three categories:

- Manufacturers of some highly toxic, dangerous, or carcinogenic products, such as asbestos, benzidine dyes, and a few pesticides have not yet been able to develop safer substitutes or to adapt their technologies to meet environmental, workplace-health, and consumer standards easily.

- In some basic mineral-processing industries (for example, copper, zinc, and lead processing), international dispersion has occurred as a result of environmental problems in combination with other changing locational incentives (raw-material availability, other nations' requirements that minerals be processed in the country where they are mined) and economic problems (low prices, high interest rates, recession).

- Finally, chemical companies may have shifted production of a very small number of chemical intermediates—that is, chemicals needed for the manufacture of other products—overseas in part because of pollution and, more significantly, workplace-health regulations.

Although The Conservation Foundation research originally focused on the impacts of pollution-control costs and of project delays caused by complex environmental regulatory requirements, the findings indicate that the handful of industries experiencing international dislocations generally have been hit harder by workplace-health standards than by pollution regulations.

III. *The increased relocation abroad of these few industries is not representative of the response by most mineral and chemical producers to environmental regulations.* No examples were found of flight from pollution or workplace-health standards in industries where product demand is expanding and U.S. producers enjoy technological superiority. Most individual mineral and chemical producers have responded to environmental regulations with technological innovations, changes in production processes or raw materials, more efficient process controls, and other adaptations that have proved more economical and less drastic than flight overseas. The few industries undergoing international dislocations because of pollution and workplace-health standards generally have also been experiencing reduced product demand, lagging technological innovation, and insufficient profit for substantial new capital investment.

The research summarized in this report indicates that the costs and logistics of complying with environmental regulations do not emerge as decisive factors when most companies select desirable countries for branch-plant locations. Neither do the regulations significantly affect the international competitiveness of most industries. There is no reason to believe that environmental regulations in the United States are significantly intensifying the major long-term trend in international industrial location—the gradual shift of many industries from the most industrialized to rapidly industrializing countries.

This finding does not mean that environmental regulations have not burdened U.S. companies; nor does it mean that environmental regulations are not important in the industrial-location process. Instead, it means that, whatever the importance of the differentials in the costs of complying with environmental regulations in industrialized and industrializing countries, they have not offset larger trends shaping aggregate international industrial-siting patterns.

Two broad policy implications are apparent from these conclusions:

- Relaxation of regulatory standards, by reducing incentives for technological progress and manufacturing-process changes, would not restore the long-term competitiveness of U.S. industries experiencing pressures for industrial flight. Rather, it would remove an important incentive for technological progress, as well as increase worker- and public-health hazards.

- Any effort within Congress or the executive branch to roll back, weaken, or fail to enforce existing environmental regulations cannot legitimately be supported by arguing that the stringency of those regulations has caused a significant amount of the United States's productive capacity in important manufacturing industries to be transferred abroad.

1. Fears of an Industrial Exodus

The multitude of new federal regulations in the 1970s forced many industries to make fundamental changes in the ways they operated in the United States. Huge capital investments were required as manufacturers adapted to new laws governing water effluents, air emissions, solid wastes, hazardous and toxic substances, and workplace health and safety. Furthermore, the labyrinth of new regulations at the federal, state, and local levels made it more difficult to build and operate production facilities in many industries, even when large amounts of money were spent on pollution controls.[1]

In many cases, the new capital and operating expenditures, as well as perceived lost opportunity costs, associated with environmental controls in the United States far exceeded those of industries operating in other nations around the world.[2] Consequently, a major concern was that the cost and logistics of complying with the new environmental regulations might undermine the competitiveness of U.S.-based firms in world trade and induce U.S. companies to locate new production facilities abroad.[3] Indeed, an economic impact study commissioned by the Manufacturing Chemists Association (now the Chemical Manufacturers Association) predicted in 1975 that passage of pending legislation to control toxic substances would lead to a transfer of industry out of the United States:

> There would be considerable emphasis toward the redirection and growth of chemical process industries abroad. Multinational firms would seriously reconsider their positions with a strong emphasis on foreign investment. Foreign producers, taking advantage of the U.S. situation, undoubtedly would increase capital, R&D [research and development] and related investment in their home countries thus effecting a further transfer of chemical industry growth as well as dominance from the U.S.[4]

Such prospects raised two major concerns in the United States. The first was that the U.S. economy and overall U.S. industrial base would be adversely affected. It was feared that employment, the balance of trade, and even national security would be threatened if substantial numbers of U.S. industrial facilities transferred production out of the United States in response to high environmental costs.[5] Second, environmental groups worried that U.S. firms would take advantage of developing countries' intense desire for industry

1

and set up factories that polluted the atmosphere and the water, ignored worker health and safety considerations, and caused other serious environmental hazards in the Third World.[6]

In recent years, the debate over whether environmental regulations are harming U.S. industry has intensified. Continuing low output and high unemployment in many large industries that have been hit with high regulatory costs have contributed to this concern, as has a growing emphasis in domestic policy debates on the need to stimulate U.S. exports and to reindustrialize this country. Frequently, environmental regulations have been blamed not only for increasing costs for U.S. consumers and for depressing the financial outlook of many domestic industries, but also for causing many industrial plants to close and thereby leading to a reduction in overall U.S. industrial capacity. These accusations prompted industry groups— and subsequently the Reagan administration—to push efforts to water down or restructure government environmental regulations during the early 1980s.[7]

THE INDUSTRIAL-FLIGHT HYPOTHESIS

In the mid-1970s, public-policy analysts and government policy makers worried that environmental regulations might induce industrial flight from the United States in three distinct (though not mutually exclusive) ways: (a) by increasing total production costs and thereby decreasing the comparative advantage of producing goods in the United States, (b) by reducing the number of sites available for industry and reducing the ease and speed with which industries could build new plants or expand old ones, and (c) by directly inhibiting the manufacture of certain products in the United States. Each of these concerns merits brief examination.

Pollution-Control Costs

Both international-trade theory and classical industrial-location theory stress that comparative costs are an important determinant of the direction of trade and the location of industrial facilities. Accordingly, it was believed that any environmental regulations that drove up the costs of producing a particular good in one country would have clear impacts on the international competitiveness of firms within that country. Sooner or later, companies with the ability to move capital investments across national boundaries would be forced to do so to remain competitive. Economists, in short, expected that if capital was mobile in an industry and if other factors remained equal, capital would migrate from countries with high environmental costs of production to those with low environmental costs of production.[8]

Ingo Walter, one of the first economists to study the international implications of environmental regulations, noted:

> We would expect environmental pressure to promote a gradual shift of pollution-intensive forms of economic activity from higher income to lower income countries internationally, with the range of activities affected gradually widening over time. This will have notable implications for the development process. . . . There may indeed be instances where the export of pollution through capital investments abroad becomes national policy in certain economic sectors, to the benefit of both capital exporting and capital importing countries.[9]

An important assumption made by economists was that multinational firms would be sensitive to environmental-control costs in their worldwide location decisions. After all, these corporations control a large percentage of world productive capacity in high-technology, high-pollution industries (for example, chemical manufacturing and petroleum refining). One textbook predicted:

> Multinational corporations . . . will be very sensitive to disparities among various states' pollution control standards, which affect production costs and competitiveness in international trade. To the extent that these disparities develop, they will have a substantial impact on investment decisions by corporations and on the trade position of various states.[10]

Thus, the changing comparative costs of environmental regulations were viewed as a potentially significant new factor in determining the international allocation of industrial production, reducing the comparative advantage of the highly industrialized nations in producing many products, and accelerating the industrial development of underindustrialized, unregulated countries.

Blockage of Plant Construction and Expansion

Concerns about the widening international gap in pollution-control costs were compounded in the late 1970s by fears that environmental regulations and public concern might also block or significantly slow construction of new plants and expansion of existing ones. Business analysts in particular worried that restricting site choices or slowing the siting process too much might lead industries simply to give up hope and move abroad.

Some of the apprehension about this problem of blockage was directed at federal regulations that did more than set pollution levels and technology requirements—for example, requirements that new or expanded plants in nonattainment areas obtain air-pollution offsets, or standards for the prevention of significant deterioration (PSD) in areas with good air quality. But it also focused on state and local land-use controls (often made stricter in response to local opposition to particular siting proposals) and on delays caused by hostile local governments, public protests, and lengthy court proceedings. Thus, Christopher J. Duerksen, a Conservation Foundation senior associate, wrote in 1979 that:

> A major factor in industrial location in the United States is local blockage of new plants, often through land use zoning controls or local referenda. Thus, an industry, in its initial selection of plant sites, may not foreclose consideration of a location in a jurisdiction or region with a reputation for strong environmental awareness, but will go elsewhere when it becomes apparent that its plant will never receive final approval due to local resistance.[11]

Some analysts predicted that such local environmental opposition was becoming so pervasive that it would produce international "spillover" effects. For example, two New York University business professors, Thomas Gladwin and Ingo Walter, claimed that environmental opposition leading to blockage was speeding up both the service orientation of developed countries and the movement of "dirty" industries to developing countries:

> It is clear that increasing environmental opposition to new manufacturing investment in many developed countries is merely reinforcing shifts toward a greater service orientation. Environmental opposition is a major factor in favoring increased relocation of industrial production to developing countries—which may have both lower environmental preferences and greater assimilative capabilities than the advanced nations.[12]

But this blockage of new industrial plants can occur even without public controversy, as John Quarles, former deputy administrator of the U.S. Environmental Protection Agency, has pointed out: "Far more likely than the public defeat of a project is the private decision never to propose it." This "mysterious and unquantifiable 'stillborn project' phenomenon" may be the most insidious of all factors inhibiting the reindustrialization of the United States, according to Quarles.[13]

Constraints on Hazardous Production

Some regulations passed in recent years, especially those governing workplace health and safety, have made it very difficult to produce certain goods at all in the United States with existing technology and production methods. As a result, concern also arose by the late 1970s that some industries were being forced overseas because they lacked the technology to meet new standards to reduce public and worker exposure to hazardous and toxic substances.

A report issued in 1978 by a private consultant, Barry Castleman, highlighted some of the industries where this phenomenon was already occurring or appeared imminent. Castleman's report, which aroused enough concern in Congress to prompt a series of hearings chaired by Representative David R. Obey (D.-Wis.), attributed plant closings in the United States and plant openings abroad in the asbestos products, zinc smelting, arsenic, benzidine dye, and pesticide industries to stringent U.S. workplace-health standards.[14]

The Castleman report contended that this phenomenon was the beginning of a long-term trend. In fact, the report concluded, "The economy of hazard export is emerging as a driving force in new plant investment in many hazardous and polluting industries."[15] Castleman boldly predicted that "in the next decade, the export of hazards from the U.S. to Third World Countries is likely to increase" and "may soon lead to wholesale exodus in major industries."[16] In addition, he listed a series of problems that widespread flight of hazardous and polluting industries away from the United States would cause:

> The international trade impacts of hazard export include export of jobs from regulating to nonregulating countries; shift of international balance of payments in favor of nonregulating countries; export of mortal health hazards and environmental destruction to workers and communities in nonregulating nations, in order to produce goods for consumption by the regulating countries; weakened competitive position of reputable manufacturers who incur control costs and compete in domestic and world markets against less scrupulous companies; prolonged widespread use of discredited, extremely hazardous technologies, arising from the continuing "subsidy" of certain industries by workers and communities exposed to uncontrolled, well-recognized, mortal health hazards; and aggravated international relations resulting from developing nations' awareness and concern over becoming dumping grounds for hazard export from industrial nations.[17]

Since 1978, several other studies and journalistic inquiries have sought to corroborate Castleman's findings and predictions and have identified numerous individual cases where factories producing substances harmful to workers have moved from the United States to countries where governmental workplace-health standards are less onerous.[18]

REACTIONS TO THE PROSPECTS OF RELOCATION

Many international economists viewed the prospects of a gradual shift of whole industrial sectors in response to environmental factors as a positive development for both developing and developed countries. They noted that the shift would contribute to overall global economic efficiency, stimulate more rapid industrial development in the Third World, and lead to a more optimal international division of labor. Indeed, most free-market economists opposed suggestions that the U.S. government either prevent corporations from moving abroad to reduce their regulatory control costs or force uniform international standards on corporations and developing countries. They argued that such actions would drive up consumer prices, frustrate the economic aspirations of developing countries, and reduce overall productive investments by corporations worldwide.[19]

In addition, theoretical economists argued that the U.S. government should not succumb to the demands of domestic producers for protection from imports produced with lower environmental-control costs than those in the United States. Ingo Walter, for example, contended that attempting "to countervail competitive advantage attributable to environmental measures is thus no more justified than similar protection designed to affect differences in capital or labor costs."[20]

The Politics of "Flight"

Not all groups have viewed the prospect of environmentally induced relocation by U.S. companies as benignly as have economists. Two domestic political coalitions, in particular, have expressed alarm at the possible implications of widespread migration by those industries most affected by pollution and workplace-safety controls.

One coalition—an amalgamation of labor unions, environmental groups, and consumer advocates—essentially argues that, in the absence of international agreements equalizing environmental controls, the U.S. government should find ways to: (a) protect U.S. firms from offshore competition by unregulated industries, (b) prevent firms from fleeing the United States to escape regulations, and (c) require U.S. companies operating overseas to abide by the same regulations and standards that they would face in the United States.[21] Many in this coalition worry that U.S. corporations threaten to relocate abroad as a means to undermine the intent of regulations and to extract concessions from developing countries.[22]

The second coalition is composed primarily of business and conservative groups that believe that many of the economic woes in the United States stem from overregulation of industry. These groups argue that environmental regulations have forced U.S. companies to move abroad and have thereby contributed to national unemployment, decreased industrial production, and balance-of-trade woes. Advocates of this view contend that many U.S. pollution-control regulations should be eased to reduce these problems.[23]

Some industry groups, however, have complained that a few unscrupulous companies have put competitive pressure on others by actively searching for countries with lax environmental regulations. These groups have called for government action to stop "underdeveloped countries being used as pollution havens by corporations seeking to evade the anti-pollution laws of the U.S. and other industrialized nations."[24]

Government policy makers have tended since the mid-1970s to operate on the assumption that environmental regulations are indeed responsible for significant declines in the competitiveness and productive capacity of U.S.-based firms, for increases in imports of manufactured products, and for increasing the number of U.S. industries locating overseas. A high-ranking official of the federal Occupational Safety and Health Administration, Dr. Joseph Wagoner, said in 1977, "The multinational implications of adhering to U.S. standards has [sic] in some cases already had the consequence of removing the dirty operations to Latin America and keeping the cleaner part of the production process here."[25]

Since the mid-1970s, Congress has repeatedly debated whether environmental regulations have forced U.S. industries overseas. Although Congress has passed no legislation specifically addressing this perceived problem, it has considered proposals to ease regulations and increase import tariffs for certain industries in the United States, and to make it more difficult for U.S. companies to close plants at home in order to build new ones abroad.[26] In addition, recent efforts in Congress to weaken the Clean Air Act and other environmental legislation have drawn support from the contention that existing laws place U.S.-based producers at a severe competitive disadvantage vis-à-vis producers operating in other countries.[27]

Government's Responses

Two successive presidential administrations have shared the perception that pollution and workplace-health regulations have prompted

U.S. companies to build more plants abroad. In response, the Carter administration tried to secure international agreements to equalize pollution-control regulations.[28] Labor Secretary Ray Marshall, for example, proposed that the United States use import tariffs to increase the price of foreign goods deemed to have been produced under conditions hazardous to workers.[29] The administration also explored possible methods of reducing industrial flight and ensuring that U.S. companies would take antipollution measures in their overseas plants.[30]

Similarly, at the Tokyo Round talks on the General Agreement on Tariffs and Trade in 1978, U.S. negotiators explicitly addressed the effects of pollution and workplace-health regulations on U.S. industry. President Carter's chief trade negotiator, Robert Strauss, urged representatives at the talks to consider pollution and workplace-health standards in light of a "pattern of flight" by industry to countries with low standards. Although he cautioned against a new protectionism, Strauss said, "American standards in these areas are among the highest in the world, and we do not want this U.S. willingness to protect the environment and our workers to disadvantage the various U.S. producers willing to pay such costs."[31]

In contrast to the Carter administration, the Reagan administration has approached the problem of industrial relocation by seeking to roll back regulations targeted by industry as burdensome, rather than by trying to bring the rest of the world up to U.S. standards.[32] As part of their overall concern about the impacts of government regulation on business activity in the United States, President Reagan's economic advisers have expressed alarm about the effects that U.S. environmental regulations have on international competitiveness. Thus, Murray L. Weidenbaum, the first chairman of the Council of Economic Advisers under President Reagan, contended:

> One result of the pressures for production processes to meet government environmental and safety requirements is that a larger share of company investment (about one-tenth at present) is being devoted to these required social responsibilities, rather than to increasing the capacity to produce a higher quantity or quality of material output, at least as conventionally measured. Coupled with the many factory closings due to regulation, these requirements are resulting in a smaller productive capacity in the American economy than is generally realized.[33]

Moreover, Weidenbaum worried,

American business does not operate in a closed society, and it finds itself more and more handicapped in competing at home and abroad with foreign companies that do not bear similarly heavy regulatory burdens. The ultimate costs of excessive government involvement in the economy can be seen in the factories that are not built, the jobs that are not created, the goods and services that are not produced, and the incomes that are not generated.[34]

One of the first steps taken by President Reagan after he assumed office in January 1981 was the establishment of a Cabinet-level Task Force on Regulatory Relief, chaired by Vice-President George Bush. In the testimony that hundreds of industry groups gave to that task force, environmental and workplace-health standards were among the regulations most often targeted as overly burdensome. Frequently, industry groups cited the loss of competitiveness by domestic production facilities as a major justification for regulatory relief and claimed that their alternative was to build more plants abroad.[35]

A NEED FOR DATA

Despite the assumptions of the Reagan and Carter administrations that industrial flight from environmental regulations has been a significant trend, most of the evidence cited to support claims of detrimental impacts continues to be anecdotal or inferential, not based on any empirical research. Despite extensive advocacy by labor, environmental, and business interest groups, policy makers have lacked reliable evidence of whether environmental regulations have been the driving force, a contributing factor, or merely incidental in international-location decisions by U.S. industries.

In the remaining chapters of this report, the U.S. industries having the most significant pollution-control problems are examined to assess whether, in fact, there is any reliable evidence that environmental regulations have pushed large numbers of U.S.-based firms abroad. In particular, the report seeks to determine: (a) how important environmental costs and lengthy environmental-permitting processes in the United States have become in comparison with the more traditional factors affecting international-location choices made by industrial firms, and (b) whether the few examples of "runaway shops" publicized by the Castleman report and media stories are representative of how most U.S.-based producers have responded to the problems imposed by extensive environmental regulations. These issues have significant bearing on critical ongoing national policy debates:

revision of the Clean Air Act, proposals for weakening other environmental regulations or for relieving particular industries from certain regulations, and proposals for stimulating reindustrialization of the United States.

REFERENCES

1. See U.S. Council on Environmental Quality, U.S. Department of Commerce, and U.S. Environmental Protection Agency, *The Economic Impact of Pollution Control: A Summary of Recent Studies* (Washington, D.C.: U.S. Government Printing Office, 1972), for an overview of early industry concerns.

2. Efforts to compare pollution-control costs for industry on a cross-national basis are reviewed in Charles Pearson and Anthony Pryor, *Environment: North and South* (New York: Wiley-Interscience, 1978), pp. 170ff.

3. This concern was expressed by policy makers, environmentalists, academics, industrialists and organized labor. For a cross section of views, see Ralph C. D'Arge and Allen V. Kneese, "Environmental Quality and International Trade," *International Organization* 26, no. 2 (Spring 1972):419-65; and Stephen P. Magee and William F. Ford, "Environmental Pollution, the Terms of Trade and Balance of Payments of the United States," *Kyklos* 30 (1972):101-18; C. Fred Bergsten, "The Threat from the Third World," in Richard N. Cooper, ed., *A Reordered World: Emerging International Economic Problems* (Washington, D.C.: Potomac Associates, 1973), p. 114; Eugene V. Coan, Julia N. Hillis, and Michael McCloskey, "Strategies for International Environmental Action: The Case for an Environmentally Oriented Foreign Policy," *Natural Resources Journal* 14, no. 1 (January 1974):94; testimony of Ralph Nader, in U.S. Senate, Committee on Public Works, Subcommittee on Air and Water Pollution, *Hearings on Economic Dislocations Resulting from Environmental Controls*, 92nd Cong., 1st sess., 1971; Ingo Walter, "Pollution and Protection: U.S. Environmental Controls on Competitive Distortions," *Weltwirtschaftliches Archiv* 110, no. 2 (1974):104-13; and Allen V. Kneese, "Environmental Pollution: Economics and Policy," *The American Economic Review* 61 (1971):153-66.

4. Foster D. Snell, Inc., "Economic Impact on Toxic Substances Control Legislation" (Report presented to the U.S. House, Committee on Interstate and Foreign Commerce, July 1975), reprinted in Alexander McRae, Leslie Whelchel, and Howard Rowland, eds., *Toxic Substances Control Sourcebook* (Germantown, Md.: Aspen Systems Corporation, 1978), p. 145.

5. See Bergsten, "The Threat from the Third World"; Magee and Ford, "Environmental Pollution"; Ralph C. D'Arge, "Trade, Environmental Controls and the Developing Economies," in *Problems of Environmental Economics* (Paris: Organization for Economic Cooperation and Development, 1972), p. 42; Horst Siebert, "Environmental Protection and International Specialization," *Weltwirtschaftliches Archiv* 110, no. 4 (1974):494-508; and Horst Siebert, "Trade and Environment," in Herbert Giersch, ed., *The International Division of Labour, Problems and Perspectives* (Tubingen, West Germany: International Symposium, 1974), pp. 108-21.

6. Coan, Hillis, and McCloskey, "Strategies for International Environmental Action"; and Marion Clawson, "Economic Development and Environmental Impact: International Aspects," in *Political Economy of Environment* (Papers presented at the United Nations Symposium at the Maison des Sciences de l'Homme, Paris, July 5-8, 1971).

7. See Louis J. Cordia, "Environmental Protection Agency," in Charles L. Heatherly, ed., *Mandate for Leadership: Policy Management in a Conservative Administration* (Washington, D.C.: The Heritage Foundation, 1981).

8. See, among many others, Wassily Leontief, "Environmental Repercussions and the Economic Structure: An Input-Output Approach," *The Review of Economics and Statistics* 52 (1970):262-71; Herbert G. Grubel, "Some Effects of Environmental Controls on International Trade: The Heckscher-Ohlin Model," in Ingo Walter, ed., *Studies in International Economics* (New York: Wiley-Interscience, 1976), pp. 9-28; Horst Siebert, "Comparative Advantage and Environmental Policy: A Note," *Zietschrift fur Nationalokonomie* 34 (1974):397-402; Richard Blackhurst, "International Trade and the Environment: A Review of the Literature and a Suggested Approach," *Economic Notes* 3, no. 2 (May-August 1974); R. Pethig, "Pollution, Welfare and Environmental Policy in the Theory of Comparative Advantage," *Journal of Environmental Economics and Management* 2 (1976):160-69; Anthony Y. C. Koo, "Environmental Repercussions and Trade Theory," *The Review of Economics and Statistics* 45, no. 2 (May 1974):235-244; and Ingo Walter, "Environmental Control and Patterns of International Trade and Investment," *Banca Nazionale del Lavoro Quarterly Review* 100 (1972):82-106.

9. Ingo Walter, "Environmental Management and the International Economic Order," in C. Fred Bergsten, ed., *The Future of the International Economic Order: An Agenda for Research* (Lexington, Mass.: D.C. Heath, 1973), p. 313.

10. David H. Blake and Robert S. Walters, *The Politics of Global Economic Relations* (Englewood Cliffs, N.J.: Prentice-Hall, 1976), p. 159. See also Thomas N. Gladwin and John G. Welles, "Environmental Policy and Multinational Corporate Strategy," in Walter, *Studies in International Economics*, pp. 177-224; and Ingo Walter, "Economic Response of Multinational Companies to Environmental Policy" (Report to the U.S. Department of Commerce, August 1976).

11. Christopher J. Duerksen, "Remodelling the U.S. Environmental and Land-Use Regulatory Process" (Paper presented at a Conference on the Role of Environmental and Land Use Regulation in Industrial Siting, Washington, D.C., sponsored by The Conservation Foundation, June 21, 1979), p. 3.

12. Thomas N. Gladwin and Ingo Walter, *Multinationals under Fire: Lessons in the Management of Conflict* (New York: Wiley-Interscience, 1980), pp. 914-15. See also Thomas N. Gladwin, "Patterns of Environmental Conflict over Industrial Facilities in the United States, 1970-78," *Natural Resources Journal* 20 (April 1980):243-274.

13. John Quarles, "Environmental Regulation and Economic Growth—Another View" (Remarks delivered to a conference on Siting New Industry, San Francisco, sponsored by The Conservation Foundation, May 23-24, 1983.)

14. Barry I. Castleman, "The Export of Hazardous Factories to Developing Nations" (Independent report issued March 7, 1978).

15. Ibid., p. 3.

16. Barry I. Castleman, "How We Export Dangerous Industries," *Business and*

Society Review (Fall 1978):7.

17. Ibid.

18. See, for example, Bob Wyrick, "Hazard Export," special 10-part series in *Newsday*, December 16-31, 1981; David C. Williams, "Hazardous Jobs Have Become One of America's Major Exports," *Los Angeles Times*, September 23, 1979; P. Sweeney, "Juarez Plant a 'Runaway' Firm?" *El Paso Times*, April 4, 1978; and Edward Flattau, "U.S. Firms Seek Refuge from Regulations," *Chicago Tribune*, June 16, 1979.

19. See references cited in notes 5 and 8.

20. Walter, "Environmental Management and the International Economic Order," p. 311.

21. See "Exporting Pollution: What Does It Cost," *Not Man Apart*, February 1976, p. 3; "Hazardous Industries Flee to Developing Countries," *Not Man Apart*, February 1976, p. 3; Helen Dewar, "Study Cites Firms' Flight to Third World to Avoid Safeguards," *Washington Post*, June 20, 1978; David R. Obey, "Export of Hazardous Industries," *Congressional Record*, June 29, 1978, pp. 3559-67; and Elizabeth Janger, "Multinationals and Jobs" (Address delivered to a seminar on Multinationals, Jobs and the Environment, Washington, D.C., October 20, 1978).

22. See Sheldon W. Samuels, "National Stewardship: Unilateral International Regulation of Occupational and Environmental Hazards; The Position of the Industrial Union Department" (Paper issued by the AFL-CIO, September 29, 1980), pp. 62-63; Herman Rebhan, "Labor Battles Hazard Export," *Multinational Monitor* 1, no. 2 (March 1980):3; Walter Cronkite, "To Save Our Industry and the Environment," *New York Times*, October 8, 1980; Barry Bluestone, Bennett Harrison, and Larry Baker, *Corporate Flight: The Causes and Consequences of Economic Dislocation* (Washington, D.C.: The National Center for Policy Alternatives, 1981); and Coan, Hillis; and McCloskey, "Strategies for International Environmental Action," p. 94.

23. For varying views on the motivations behind the push for deregulation, see Murray L. Weidenbaum, *The Future of Business Regulation* (New York: AMACOM, 1979); Alan Stone, *Regulation and Its Alternatives* (Washington, D.C.: Congressional Quarterly Press, 1982); Michael Pertschuk, *Revolt against Regulation* (Berkeley, Calif.: University of California Press, 1983); John L. Palmer and Isabel V. Sawhill, eds., *The Reagan Experiment* (Washington, D.C.: The Urban Institute, 1982); Peter Duignan and Alvin Rabushka, eds., *The United States in the 1980s* (Palo Alto, Calif.: Hoover Institution, 1980).

24. D. H. Dawson, Chemical Manufacturers Association, July 23, 1975, cited in Samuels, "National Stewardship," p. 63.

25. Joseph Wagoner, interview with the North American Congress on Latin America, December 1977, quoted in "Dying for Work: Occupational Health and Asbestos," *NACLA Report* 12, no. 2 (March-April 1978), p. 21.

26. Congress originally expressed its anxiety in the Federal Water Pollution Act Amendments of 1972, which directed the U.S. Department of Commerce to study the competitive impact of environmental regulations on U.S. companies. The amendments also required the president, as a means of heading off any competitive disadvantages, to "undertake to enter into international agreements to apply uniform standards of performance for the control of the discharge and emission of pollutants from new sources" through multilateral treaties, the United Nations,

and other international forums. Public Law 92-500 (October 18, 1972); 86 Stat. 897-98. See also U.S. Senate, *Hearings on Economic Dislocations*.

27. See Lawrence Mosher, "The Clean Air You're Breathing May Cost Hundreds of Billions of Dollars," *National Journal*, October 10, 1981.

28. See Sanford E. Gaines, "The Extraterritorial Reach of U.S. Environmental Legislation and Regulations," in Seymour J. Rubin and Thomas R. Graham, *Environment and Trade: The Relation of International Trade and Environmental Policy* (Totowa, N.J.: Allanheld, Osmun, 1982).

29. *Barron's*, January 16, 1978, p. 1.

30. See Charles Pearson, "An Environmental Code of Conduct for Multinational Companies," in Rubin and Graham, *Environment and Trade*.

31. Quoted in *Environment Reporter* 9, no. 10 (July 7, 1978):451. Most of these initiatives by the Carter administration failed, largely because of strong opposition from the business community and foreign countries.

32. See Susan J. Tolchin and Martin Tolchin, *Dismantling America: The Rush to Deregulate* (Boston: Houghton Mifflin, 1983). See also Lawrence Mosher, "Reaganites, with OMB List in Hand, Take Dead Aim at EPA's Regulations," *National Journal*, February 14, 1981; and S. Scheible, "Regulatory Relief," *Barron's*, June 8, 1981.

33. Murray L. Weidenbaum, "Government Power and Business Performance," in Duignon and Rabushka, *United States in the 1980s*, p. 203.

34. Ibid., pp. 209-10.

35. See especially Chemical Manufacturers Association, "Response to the Vice President and Recommendations for Regulatory Reform," summary and 2 vols. (Submissions to the Task Force on Regulatory Relief, May 1, 1981).

36. See two books by Christopher J. Duerksen, *Dow vs. California: A Turning Point in the Envirobusiness Struggle* (Washington, D.C.: The Conservation Foundation, 1982); and *Environmental Regulation of Industrial Plant Siting: How to Make It Work Better* (Washington, D.C.: The Conservation Foundation, 1983).

2. Foreign Investments and U.S. Imports by High-Pollution Industries

In recent years, many studies have tried to assess the direct macroeconomic effects of environmental regulations on gross national product, inflation, unemployment, and productivity. Most of the studies have concluded that environmental regulations have contributed incrementally but not fundamentally to general inflation rates, high unemployment in certain industries, and a slowdown in productivity growth in some industries. Even Christopher DeMuth, the former executive director of the Task Force on Regulatory Relief set up by President Reagan, has said:

> Clearly, if the new regulatory controls have been a substantial cause of our flagging measured productivity they have also reduced our competitiveness in international markets. Such evidence as can be reduced to numbers, however, fails to convict the newer regulatory programs of being major culprits in diminishing U.S. competitiveness. . . . [U.S.] experience with costly environmental and workplace controls is not radically different from that of our major competitors. Nor do available statistics suggest that regulation has been a dominant cause of our declining productivity growth.[1]

Some attempts have also been made to examine the less direct effects of environmental regulations—especially whether and how they have altered rates of capital formation in major industrial sectors.[2] This second type of inquiry has proven more problematic since no macroeconomic model or set of indicators can measure forgone investment, much less whether environmental regulations might be responsible. It may be true, as Brookings Institution economist Robert W. Crandall contends, that the maze of environmental regulations is not conducive to new investment.[3] Yet it is not clear how much more (if any) major capital investment would have taken place during the past decade if there had been no regulatory encumbrances.[4] Do the regulatory expenses and difficulties only slow and deflect new plant investments *in the short run*, or do they reduce total investments made *in the long run*? The question is impossible to answer unequivocally. Thus, John Quarles, now a prominent environmental attorney, recently noted: "The basic question is whether these regulatory impacts—both the delays and uncertainties of permit processing, and also the actual increases in construction costs—are significantly inhibiting the reindustrialization of America. One yearns for data, but no data exist."[5]

Obviously, these problems in determining whether investments are being permanently forgone in the United States because of environmental regulations make it difficult to answer the ancillary question of whether environmental factors have caused industries to locate overseas rather than in the United States. This second question is further complicated by the fact that foreign investments by U.S. companies are undertaken for many reasons unrelated to regulations. Although figures on overseas investments by U.S. corporations are readily available, they offer no clues why the investments were made. Comparative costs for environmental regulations are available for the United States and many other countries, but the costs cannot be presumed to have affected flows of capital investment unless they are examined alongside all other factors that determine industrial location. Moreover, indexes of the number of new plants that have been cancelled or delayed, or old plants that have been shut down, in the United States because of environmental regulations do not necessarily tell whether greater overseas investment has ensued. Clearly, no single methodological approach is sufficient to determine whether investments made overseas by U.S. companies can be linked to U.S. environmental regulations.

Another problem, of course, is that regulations have not affected all industries or groups of industries in the same way. Some industries have clearly borne a disproportionate share of pollution-control costs, public opposition to new plants, and workplace-safety requirements. Thus, examining aggregate statistics for industry in general will not reveal problems in particular manufacturing sectors.

This point was emphasized by a 1979 Conservation Foundation study of direct investment in foreign countries by U.S. firms during the 1970s. In that study, no evidence was found that "environmental dislocation" was altering *overall* U.S. industry investment patterns: "Although the volume of foreign investments by American corporate affiliates has continued to grow during the 1970's, overall investment patterns do not appear to have been different than they would have been if the United States had not undergone a revolution in its environmental standards."[6]

To overcome the shortcomings of relying on any one set of indicators, or examining only aggregate statistics covering all industries, this chapter utilizes a variety of methods to ascertain whether environmental regulations may have been instrumental in increasing overseas investment by certain "hard-hit" U.S. industries. First, it identifies those broad industrial sectors that (a) have been hardest hit by U.S. environmental regulations, (b) are sufficiently footloose to invest abroad in response to changing short- and medium-term circumstances, and (c) have not based their recent locational decisions on a specific set of overwhelming factors unrelated to environmental concerns. Then, for the sectors that appear most susceptible to dislocations caused by environmental regulations, the chapter examines foreign investment and trade figures for the past decade to identify any large increases or changing trends that coincide with the predicted effects of U.S. environmental regulations.

INDUSTRIAL SECTORS MOST SUSCEPTIBLE TO RELOCATION

Identifying the industrial sectors that have been hardest hit by environmental regulations is fairly easy, since the same industries have tended to be faced with all three of the problems identified in chapter 1: high pollution-control costs, blockage of plant construction and expansion, and production restrictions in response to workplace hazards. Four broad manufacturing sectors—mineral processing,* chemicals, pulp and paper, and petroleum production—have paid between two-thirds and three-fourths of all annual capital expenditures for pollution control by manufacturing industries in recent years (figures 2.1 and 2.2). All four of these sectors have tended to incur higher-than-average pollution-control expenditures in proportion to total new plant and capital expenditures, as figure 2.3 illustrates. No other grouping of manufacturing industries has been above or even close to the average.

These manufacturing sectors—along with the nonmanufacturing sectors of mineral mining, electric utilities, and nuclear power plants—turned up most frequently in a study by Thomas Gladwin and Ingo Walter of 366 industry-related environmental conflicts during the 1970s. Furthermore, all of the industries that the Castleman

---

*In this chapter, all aggregate data on the mineral-processing sector include manufacturing industries involved in smelting, refining, and otherwise processing primary and fabricated metals and major nonmetallic minerals. The data exclude basic mining industries, which are not considered manufacturing industries. Also omitted are the stone, clay, glass, and cement industries; government statistics often lump data for these industries together in an "other manufacturing industries" category.

18

**Figure 2.1
Plant and Equipment Expenditures
for Pollution Control, 1973–1982**

Billion dollars

————— All manufacturing industries

------- Combined 4 high-pollution sectors

1973 1974 1975 1976 1977 1978 1979 1980 1981 1982

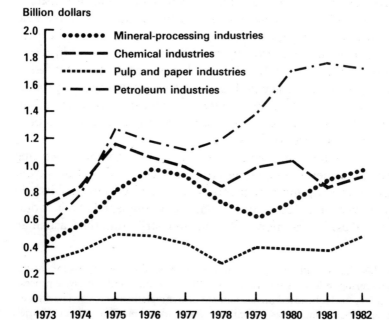

Billion dollars

•••••• Mineral-processing industries

— — — Chemical industries

·········· Pulp and paper industries

—·—·— Petroleum industries

1973 1974 1975 1976 1977 1978 1979 1980 1981 1982

Source: Gary L. Rutledge and Betsy D. O'Conner, "Plant and Equipment Expenditures by Business for
   Pollution Abatement, 1973–80 and Planned 1981," *Survey of Current Business* 61, no. 6 (June 1981);
   and "Plant and Equipment Expenditures by Business for Pollution Abatement, 1981 and Planned 1982,"
   Survey of Current Business 62, no. 6 (June 1982).

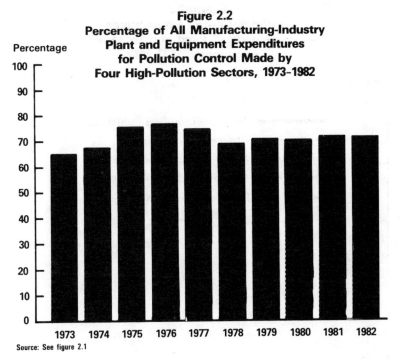

Figure 2.2
Percentage of All Manufacturing-Industry
Plant and Equipment Expenditures
for Pollution Control Made by
Four High-Pollution Sectors, 1973–1982

Percentage

Source: See figure 2.1

report (discussed in chapter 1) cited as experiencing locational problems because of workplace hazards fell within either the mineral-processing or chemical sector.

In its analysis of recent foreign investment and import trends in this select group of industrial sectors, this chapter includes, as part of the chemical industries, the portion of the petroleum-production sector concerned with downstream petrochemicals (for example, petroleum-based chemical products and petrochemical feedstocks). The other broad group in the petroleum sector—the basic petroleum producers, including storage and transport facilities and petroleum refineries—is omitted from the investigation. Even though these producers have experienced high pollution-control costs and difficulties in building new plants, it is impractical to factor out all the extraordinary international circumstances that have affected oil refiners during the past decade.*

---

*In fact, to ensure that changes affecting the basic petroleum producers do not obscure or overshadow the trade and investment data included in this chapter, none of the statistics presented here include petroleum refining as a manufacturing industry or petroleum products as manufactured goods.

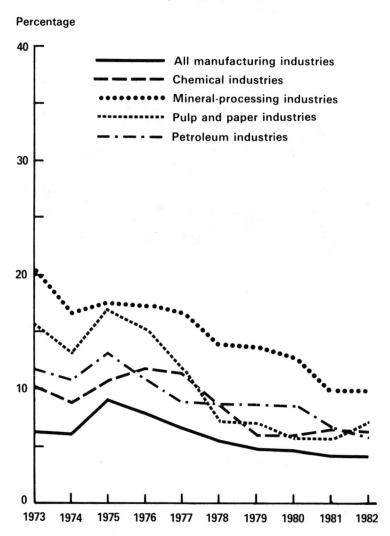

**Figure 2.3
Pollution-Control Expenditures
as Percentage of Plant and Equipment
Expenditures, 1973-1982**

Percentage

All manufacturing industries
Chemical industries
Mineral-processing industries
Pulp and paper industries
Petroleum industries

Source: See figure 2.1.

FOREIGN INVESTMENT AND IMPORT TRENDS

Many factors affect the location decisions of specific industries and individual firms. As a result, statistics on foreign investments and imports do not necessarily indicate how important environmental factors have become to high-pollution manufacturing sectors making those choices. However, analyzing foreign-investment and import trends for those industries—mineral processing, chemicals (including petrochemicals), and pulp and paper—is a good starting point. At least, such an analysis can indicate whether trends are moving in the direction that would be expected if environmental concerns had gained a predominant place in international industrial-location decisions.

If environmental regulations are causing an exodus of high-pollution industries from the United States, several trends should be quite pronounced:

- Foreign direct investment should be increasing more rapidly for the three high-pollution manufacturing sectors than for other manufacturing industries.
- U.S. imports of minerals, chemicals, and pulp and paper products should be expanding faster than overall manufactured imports.
- Less-developed countries (LDCs) should be increasing their share of foreign direct investment by high-pollution manufacturers, since most developed countries now have environmental-regulatory systems as stringent, or nearly as stringent, as the U.S. system.
- An increasing share of U.S. imports of goods produced by high-pollution industries should be coming from the LDCs.

The existence of these trends would not prove that environmental factors are their cause, but an absence of the trends would provide strong evidence that environmental factors have not gained the prominence in location decisions that many analysts predicted.

The extent to which industrial-location patterns over the past decade have conformed to these trends can be seen by examining three sets of data that are generally available, consistent, and broken down by broad industry groupings: the total value of foreign direct investments by U.S. companies; annual capital expenditures abroad by U.S companies; and U.S. imports of manufactured products. By using these figures to compare the three pollution-intensive manufacturing sectors with other manufacturing industries, it can be seen whether direct investments in foreign countries and U.S. imports are growing faster for the mineral-processing, chemical, and pulp and paper sectors than for other industries. These figures can also indicate whether LDCs, which typically have environmental regulations significantly weaker than those in the United States, are grabbing larger shares of U.S. overseas investments by high-pollution sectors and of U.S. imports of products manufactured by those sectors.

High-Pollution Industries Compared with All U.S. Manufacturing Industries

Investments

During a decade of rapid increases in the overall value of foreign direct investment by U.S. manufacturing industries, the mineral-processing and chemical industries slightly increased their combined share of total U.S. overseas manufacturing investment. Comparable foreign-investment figures are not available for pulp and paper.

Figure 2.4 indicates that the value of all foreign direct investment by U.S. manufacturing industries rose from $44.37 billion in 1973 to $92.48 billion in 1981. By the same token, the total value for foreign direct investments by the mineral-processing and chemical industries went up from $11.39 billion in 1973 to $25.34 billion in 1981. Although overseas investment by chemical industries grew at a rate only slightly faster than the average of all manufacturing industries, the mineral-processing industries nearly tripled the value of their foreign direct investment during these years. These increases by the mineral-processing and chemical industries boosted the two sectors' combined share of total foreign direct investment by U.S. manufacturing industries from 25.7 percent in 1973 to 28.4 percent in 1980 (figure 2.5).

Annual Capital Expenditures

U.S. manufacturers in the three high-pollution sectors had higher year-by-year overseas capital expenditures in the second half of the 1970s than they did in the first. However, those companies' annual expenditures increased significantly more slowly than did the expenditures of manufacturing industries in general and tapered off in the early 1980s (figure 2.6). As a consequence, the high-pollution industries' percentage of total annual overseas capital expenditures by

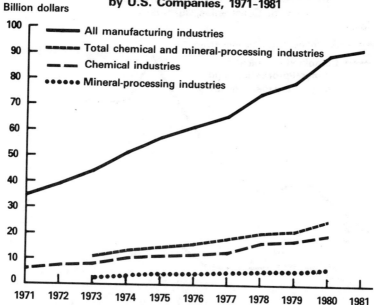

Figure 2.4
Foreign Direct Investment
by U.S. Companies, 1971–1981

Billion dollars

— All manufacturing industries
▬▬▬ Total chemical and mineral-processing industries
— — Chemical industries
•••••• Mineral-processing industries

Data indicate cumulative values. Data for 1971-1972 not available for mineral-processing industries and for combined chemical and mineral-processing industries.

Source: "U.S. Direct Investment Abroad, selected years," *Survey of Current Business,* published annually in August edition.

Figure 2.5
Percentage of Foreign Direct Investment
by U.S. Manufacturing Industries Occupied by
Chemical and Mineral-Processing Sectors,
1973–1980

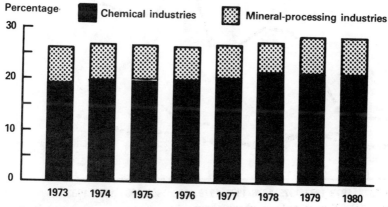

Percentage   ■ Chemical industries   ▨ Mineral-processing industries

Source: See figure 2.4.

24

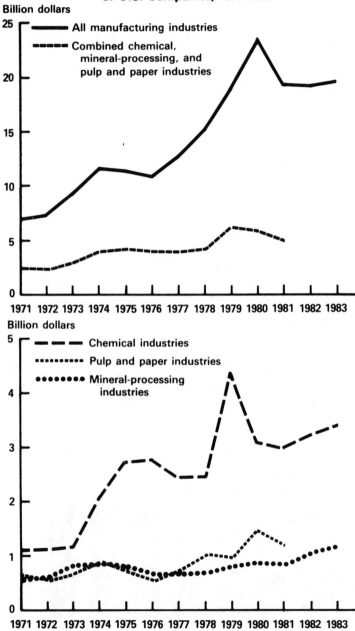

Figure 2.6
Annual Capital Expenditures
by Majority-Owned Foreign Affiliates
of U.S. Companies, 1971–1983

Data for 1982–1983 not available for pulp and paper industries.

Source: "Capital Expenditures by Majority-Owned Foreign Affiliates of U.S. Companies,"
Survey of Current Business, published annually in October edition.

U.S. manufacturing industries has averaged lower in recent years than it did in the early 1970s (figure 2.7).

These figures are most significant because widespread industrial flight abroad by U.S. high-pollution industries would register first in large increases in annual overseas capital expenditures (for building new industrial plants) and only gradually over time would cumulate to affect the total value of U.S. foreign direct investments. Thus, since annual spending overseas has been expanding more slowly for the three high-pollution industries than it has for manufacturing industries overall, there is no reason to believe that large jumps in the shares of total foreign direct investment held by these industries are in the offing through the mid-1980s.

U.S. Imports

If environmental regulations were inducing more U.S. industries to shift production facilities abroad, the imports of goods produced by the high-pollution sectors would presumably be increasing at a faster pace than would otherwise be expected. As can be seen in figure 2.8, the total value of U.S. imports of manufactured goods grew from approximately $46 billion in 1971 to about $261 billion in 1981 (an increase of more than fivefold), while the value of imported chemicals, processed minerals, and pulp and paper went from just under $9 billion to about $37 billion (a more than fourfold increase). The value of chemical imports, which account for almost three-fourths of the high pollution imports (in dollar value), quadrupled between 1971 and 1981, while the value of pulp and paper imports more than tripled. Only imports of processed minerals expanded faster than all manufactured imports, leaping sixfold in value. However, since this sector accounts for only about one-seventh of the total value of high-pollution imports, the share of all high-pollution goods shrank from 19.0 percent of the total value of U.S. manufactured imports in 1971 to 14.2 percent by 1981 (figure 2.9).

For the purposes of this report, an even better set of figures than overall U.S. manufactured imports is the subset of these imports sent from abroad by affiliates of U.S.-based companies. However, data on exports to the United States by overseas U.S. affiliates have not been collected annually by the U.S. Department of Commerce since 1977. To delineate a reasonable trend line, then, figures 2.10 and 2.11 show the years 1966-76 for the mineral-processing and chemical industries. Once again, separate data are not available for the pulp and paper industries.

26

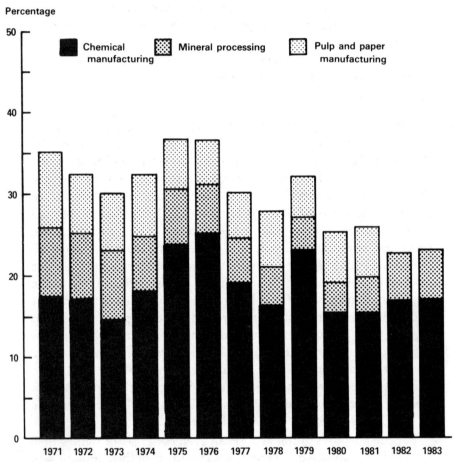

Figure 2.7
Percentage of High-Pollution Sectors
in Annual Capital Expenditures by
Majority-Owned Foreign Affiliates
of U.S. Companies, 1971-1983

Percentage

Data for pulp and paper manufacturing for 1982-1983 not available.

Source: See figure 2.6.

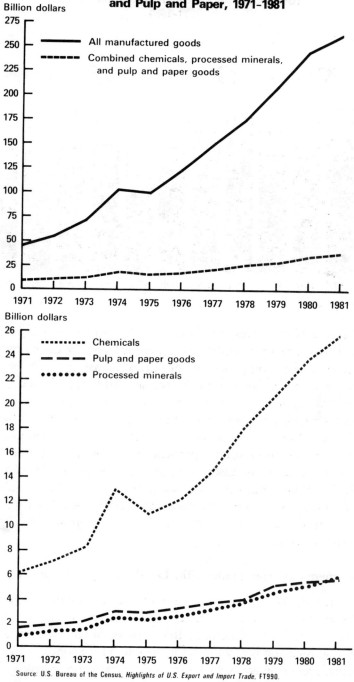

Figure 2.8
U.S. Imports of All Manufactured Goods and of Chemicals, Processed Minerals, and Pulp and Paper, 1971–1981

Source: U.S. Bureau of the Census, *Highlights of U.S. Export and Import Trade,* FT990.

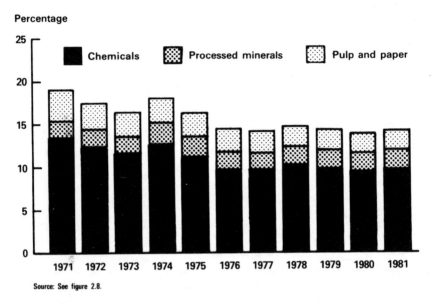

**Figure 2.9
Percentage of Chemicals, Processed
Minerals, and Pulp and Paper in
Total U.S. Imports of Manufactured Goods,
1971–1981**

Percentage

■ Chemicals ▨ Processed minerals ▫ Pulp and paper

Source: See figure 2.8.

Figure 2.10 indicates that between 1966 and 1976 the value of chemicals and processed minerals sent to the United States by overseas affiliates of U.S. companies did not grow as fast as the value of all manufactured goods sent by U.S. overseas affiliates. However, once again, the separate figures for the mineral-processing sector differ from the aggregate trend: the value of processed minerals sent to the United States by overseas affiliates did grow faster than the value of all manufactured goods, particularly between 1970 and 1976. Although the rapid increases in imports of minerals processed abroad by U.S. affiliates have not been large enough to offset the slower-than-average increases for chemical imports (figure 2.11), they point to the need for further investigation of the mineral-processing industries (see chapter 3).

Investments in, and Trade with, Less-Developed Countries

Most developed countries now have environmental regulatory systems that are as stringent, or nearly as stringent, as the U.S. system. In addition, although differences remain in the comparative costs that regulations in various Organization for Economic Cooperation and Development (OECD) countries impose on industries, these

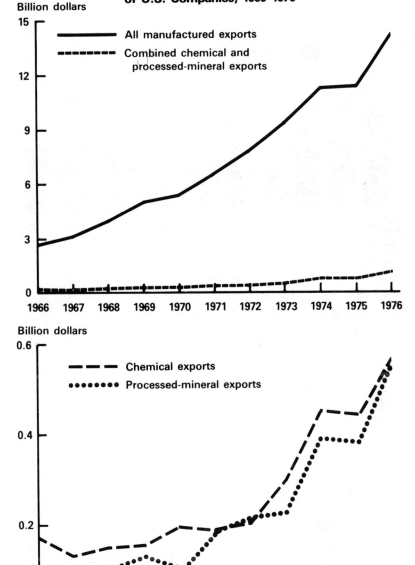

Figure 2.10
Exports to the United States by
Majority-Owned Foreign Affiliates
of U.S. Companies, 1966–1976

Separate figures for pulp and paper exports not available.

Source: "Sales by Majority Owned Foreign Affiliates of U.S. Companies," *Survey of Current Business,* published annually through 1977 in August editions.

Figure 2.11
Percentage of Chemicals and Processed Minerals
in Total Manufactured Goods Exported to the
United States by Majority-Owned Foreign Affiliates
of U.S. Companies, 1966–1976

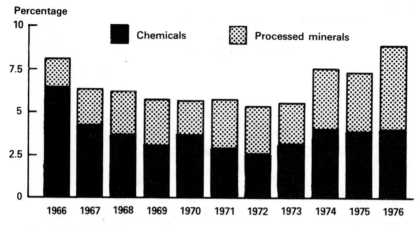

Separate figures for pulp and paper exports not available.

Source: See figure 2.10.

differences are not generally regarded as substantial enough to affect the economics of location from one OECD country to another.[7] The more substantial differences in stringency and cost of regulations are between the broad group of countries considered to be developed and those often referred to as less-developed.[*8]

Thus, another indicator of possible widespread flight from U.S. environmental regulations would be a shift in recent years to substantially more investment in LDCs by high-pollution U.S. industries and a complementary rapid increase in the LDC share of U.S. imports of goods produced by those industries.

Investments

From 1973 to 1980, the LDC share of all U.S. foreign investment by manufacturing industries climbed slowly upward from 17.6 per-

---

*In this section, the term *less-developed countries* refers to all countries excepting those belonging to the Organization for Economic Cooperation and Development (OECD). Although such a broad category includes "middle-income" countries such as several of the centrally planned economies of Eastern Europe and the oil-exporting nations of the Middle East, as well as the more affluent nations of Latin America and the Far East, most observers (see note 7) feel that outside of the OECD countries the stringency of pollution-control regulations falls off sharply. Hence, this distinction is seen as the most logical for this inquiry.

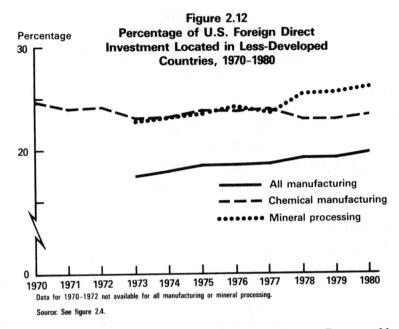

Figure 2.12
Percentage of U.S. Foreign Direct Investment Located in Less-Developed Countries, 1970–1980

Percentage

- All manufacturing
- - - Chemical manufacturing
••••••• Mineral processing

Data for 1970–1972 not available for all manufacturing or mineral processing.

Source: See figure 2.4.

cent to 19.8 percent (figure 2.12). The chemical sector fluctuated but finished the 1970s with a slightly *lower* share of its total foreign investment going to LDCs than had gone to them in 1970. The percentage of investment by U.S. mineral-processing industries in LDCs climbed steadily during this time, from 22.8 percent of the total overseas investment in 1973 to 26.2 percent by 1980. Pulp and paper figures are not available as a separate category.

Annual Capital Expenditures

In figure 2.13, the percentage of annual overseas expenditures by U.S. companies in LDCs is presented. In the early 1970s, the percentage of chemical-industry annual expenditures going to LDCs was almost identical with the percentage of expenditures by manufacturing industries overall, but a rather sharp divergence occurred after 1976, with the chemical industry sending a substantially higher percentage of its overseas expenditures to LDCs. Similarly, the mineral-processing industry actually sent a dwindling proportion of its annual overseas expenditures to LDCs in the early 1970s, although the percentage rose after 1975 and has shot upward in the first half of the 1980s. More than 40 percent of the industry's overseas capital expenditures went to LDCs in 1982 and 1983. In contrast, in every

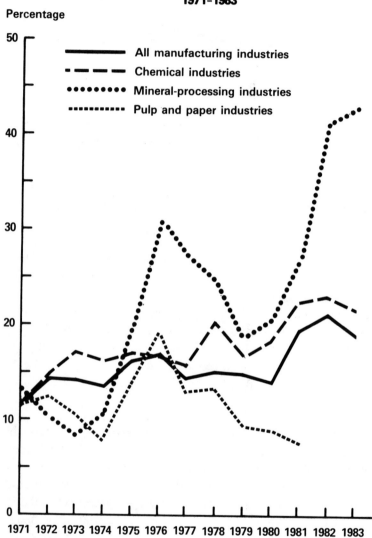

**Figure 2.13
Percentage of Annual Overseas
Capital Expenditures by U.S. Affiliates
Going to Less-Developed Countries,
1971–1983**

Percentage

All manufacturing industries
Chemical industries
Mineral-processing industries
Pulp and paper industries

Data for 1982–1983 not available for pulp and paper industries.

Source: See figure 2.6.

year of the 1970s except 1976, the percentage of annual overseas expenditures by U.S. pulp and paper companies going to LDCs was lower than the comparable percentage for overall U.S. manufacturing industry investments.

U.S. Imports

Between 1972 and 1981, the LDCs as a group steadily increased their share of total manufactured imports to the United States—from about 28 percent to just over 36 percent. As can be seen in figure 2.14, imports of manufactured chemicals from LDCs failed to reflect this trend, declining as a share of total U.S. chemical imports during the same time period. However, the LDC share of imported processed minerals expanded even faster than did the LDC share of total manufactured imports. Although pulp and paper imports from LDCs did jump up dramatically in 1978 and 1980, they remained under 5 percent of total pulp and paper imports in most years. Since total U.S. pulp and paper imports are small, and since over 90 percent of those imports continue to come from Canada, the aberrations that show in the percentage figures during 1978 and 1980 do not represent significant trends.

CONCLUSIONS

The aggregate data on recent overseas investment and import patterns by the U.S. high-pollution industries yield three broad conclusions. First, during the past decade of very high pollution costs and logistical problems in complying with complex environmental regulations, the overall foreign-investment and import trends of the mineral-processing, chemical, and pulp and paper industries—the three sectors most likely to have been pushed abroad to escape such regulations—have not differed fundamentally from those of U.S. manufacturing industries in general. Since these industries show no large increases in total overseas foreign investment, no large shifts to developing countries, and no large jumps in imports of their pollution-intensive goods, there is no reason to believe that environmental regulations are causing a widespread exodus of U.S. industry.

Second, several slight shifts at the margin nevertheless can be detected in the overall trends. These shifts deserve further study:

- The investment data for the U.S. mineral-processing industries indicate small but consistent upward adjustments in the total

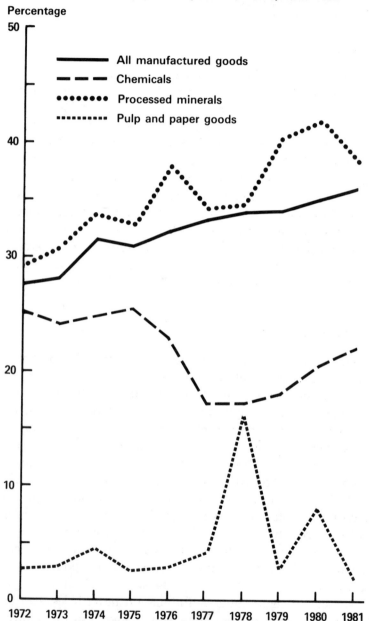

Figure 2.14
Percentage of U.S. Imports Coming
from Less-Developed Countries, 1972–1981

Percentage

—— All manufactured goods
– – – Chemicals
•••••• Processed minerals
·········· Pulp and paper goods

Source: Computed from figures derived from U.S. Bureau of the Census, *Highlights of U.S. Export and Import Trends,* FT990, December issues; and U.S. Department of Commerce, "U.S. Trade with Major World Areas," *Overseas Business Reports,* periodic.

value of overseas investment, annual overseas expenditures, and percentage of overseas investment going to the LDCs. Similar advances occurred in U.S. imports of processed minerals, both overall and from LDCs. Although total investments by the mineral-processing industries are only about one-third of those by the chemical producers, these shifts could be significant if they continue. These trends certainly parallel those that would be expected if environmental regulations were affecting the comparative competitive advantage of U.S.-based mineral processors. But the figures in this section only indicate that U.S. producers have been increasing their investments abroad and sending growing amounts of processed minerals to the United States. They do not establish any causal relationship between these trends and U.S. environmental regulations.

- The aggregate data show no abrupt or large changes in the overseas investment or import patterns of the chemical industries. However, because of wide variations within this sector, some individual industries could have experienced substantial increases in overseas investments and in U.S. imports without skewing the aggregate data. Indeed, the increased percentage of chemical-industry annual overseas expenditures going to LDCs since 1976 might be an indication that a few specific chemical products are being produced more and more in LDCs. Once again, a closer look at the chemical sector is necessary to determine the cause of this emerging shift.

- In contrast, the aggregate data provide substantial evidence that the pulp and paper sector of U.S. manufacturing industries has not experienced widespread locational disruptions because of environmental regulations. One reason is that the pollution problems of paper companies, unlike other industries, appear to have been met fairly easily with a one-time installation of capital equipment, as is apparent from the rapid drop in pollution-control expenditures as a percentage of total capital expenditures between 1975 and 1981. On the basis of these conclusions, the pulp and paper sector is not examined further in this report.

Finally, the statistics do not indicate whether environmental regulations, alone or in tandem with other factors, have caused the trends identified in this chapter. Clearly, pollution-control expenditures remain only a small portion of total capital costs for the pollution-intensive sectors examined here. Thus, environmental-control costs cannot be examined in a vacuum. Even if environmental-control costs could be completely eliminated in some foreign country, the total savings would not be very significant—ranging from 6.3 percent for the chemical industries to 9.7 percent for the mineral-processing industries in 1982, as was seen in figure 2.3. Besides, as the Commerce Department has pointed out, even when environmental-control costs can be minimized overseas, total costs for plant construction and operation generally run much higher abroad than in the United States.[9]

Moreover, as business analysts and corporate decision makers have recognized, overseas investment decisions are heavily influenced by considerations other than production costs. Access to markets, raw-material supplies, political stability, availability of infrastructure and skilled labor, and quality-of-life considerations for executives are some of the more important of these. Put in context, then, environmental-control costs are less than one-fifth of capital costs, which are, in turn, only a portion of total production costs (along with labor, raw materials, transportation, etc.). And total costs are only one of the many tangible and intangible factors that determine whether a firm chooses to set up a production facility in the United States or overseas.

To determine how influential environmental regulations have become in determining whether industries in the two sectors remain in the United States or move abroad, chapters 3 and 4 analyze specific industries within the mineral-processing and chemical sectors that have experienced both environmental problems in the United States and declines in U.S. production or increases in imports from abroad. They identify some industries for which environmental factors have emerged as a dominant element in location decisions—either because regulations have banned or sharply curtailed production of a certain product in the United States or because public and labor-union concern have created inhospitable climates in many parts of the country. Those chapters also look at some industries that recently have increased their movement overseas because of the combined influences of environmental regulations; general public concern about pollution, health, and safety; marketing opportunities; and the availability of foreign raw materials.

REFERENCES

1. Christopher DeMuth, "Domestic Regulation and International Competitiveness" (Paper presented at conference on U.S. productivity, Brown University, February 27-28, 1981). For results of recent empirical analyses, see Gregory

Christianson, Frank Gollop, and Robert Haveman, *Environmental and Health/ Safety Regulations, Productivity Growth and Economic Performance* (Washington, D.C.: Office of Technology Assessment, 1980); *Cost of Government Regulation Study* (New York: The Business Roundtable, 1979); Robert W. Crandall, "Pollution Controls and Productivity Growth in Basic Industries," in T. Cowing and R. Stevenson, eds., *Productivity Measurement in Regulated Industries* (New York: Academic Press, 1981); Edward Denison, "Pollution Abatement Programs: Estimates of Their Effect upon Output per Unit, *Survey of Current Business* 59, no. 8 (August 1979). A number of statistical studies have estimated the macro-effects of environmental regulation on the economy: Chase Econometrics issued a study in 1976 estimating that pollution control increased the Consumer Price Index (CPI) marginally—about 0.03 percent per year; a 1979 Data Resources estimate put this figure at 0.02 percent; and the Council on Wage and Price Stability concluded in 1979 that all government regulations (for example, economic and social) added 0.075 percent to the CPI annually.

2. Peter K. Clark, *Issues in the Analysis of Capital Formation and Productivity Growth,* Brookings Papers on Economic Activity (Washington, D.C.: Brookings Institution, 1979); *Federal Regulation of New Industrial Plants* (Washington, D.C.: The American Bar Association, 1980); Robert H. Haveman and V. Kerry Smith, "Investment, Inflation, Unemployment and the Environment," in Paul R. Portnoy, ed., *Current Issues in U.S. Environmental Policy* (Washington, D.C.: Johns Hopkins University Press, 1979), p. 164; Henry M. Peskin, Paul R. Portnoy, and Allan V. Kneese, eds., *Environmental Regulation and the U.S. Economy* (Baltimore, Md.: Johns Hopkins University Press, 1981); and *Workshop on Effects of Environmental Regulation on Industrial Compliance Costs and Technological Innovation,* PRA Reports 83-9 and 83-10 (Washington, D.C.: National Science Foundation, 1983).

3. Crandall, "Pollution Controls and Productivity Growth," p. 368.

4. Crandall himself, in another article, makes this point, saying: "It is very difficult to measure opportunities foregone": Robert W. Crandall, "Regulation and Productivity Growth," in *The Decline in Productivity Growth* (Proceedings of a conference held in June 1980), Federal Reserve Bank of Boston Conference Series no. 22.

5. John Quarles, "Environmental Regulation and Economic Growth—Another View" (Remarks delivered to a conference on Siting New Industry, San Francisco, sponsored by The Conservation Foundation, May 23-24, 1983).

6. H. Jeffrey Leonard and Christopher J. Duerksen, "Environmental Regulations and the Location of Industry: An International Perspective," *Columbia Journal of World Business* 15, no. 2 (Summer 1980):56. An earlier version of this paper was presented at the Conference on the Role of Environmental and Land Use Regulation in Industrial Siting, Washington, D.C, sponsored by The Conservation Foundation, June 21, 1979. These findings have been supported by a number of studies in recent years. See Thomas N. Gladwin and John G. Welles, "Environmental Policy and Multinational Corporate Strategy," in Ingo Walter, ed., *Studies in International Environmental Economics* (New York: Wiley-Interscience, 1976); Charles Pearson and Anthony Pryor, *Environment: North and South* (New York: Wiley-Interscience, 1978), pp. 170ff.; "Corporate Investment and Production Decisions: Does Environmental Legislation Play a Role," *Economist Intelligence*

Report, November 1978; and "Environmental Factors Seen Rarely Decisive in Site Selection," *International Environment Reporter* 1, no. 5 (May 19, 1978):142. The Gladwin and Welles study, after reviewing behavioral characteristics of several firms, the factors that generally weigh heavily in foreign direct investment (FDI) decisions, and the current empirical evidence, concluded:

> Flows of foreign direct investment do not appear, as yet, to differ substantially from what would be expected in the absence of environmentally-induced shifts except in a few instances. More importantly, we do not expect a flow of environment-induced FDI of any real significance to materialise in the future. . . . A slight shift at the margin has, indeed, been introduced into the locational calculus of FDI, but for most MNCs (multinational corporations) the shift will not be significant enough to counterbalance the higher costs and risks involved in seeking out a developing nation "pollution haven" for major new facilties. MNCs will of course try to locate in areas in which all costs . . . are minimized. FDI will, of course, continue to flow to developing nations, especially those with stable governments and indigenous natural resources, but for intrinsic reasons largely unrelated to lower environmental costs. (p. 202)

In addition, interview studies with corporate officials in the United States and Europe have demonstrated that environmental factors are almost never predominant in selecting locations at home or abroad. See Howard Stafford, *The Effects of Environmental Regulations on Industrial Location*, Report on National Science Foundation Grant no. SES-8024562 (Cincinnati: Department of Geography, University of Cincinnati, June 1983); and Gabrielle Knödgen, "Environmental Regulations and the Location of Industry in Europe" (Paper presented at a conference on Siting New Industry, San Francisco, sponsored by The Conservation Foundation, May 23-24, 1983).

7. See Michel Potier, "Trade, Competitiveness and Environment: A Discussion," in Walter, *Studies in International Environmental Economics*, pp. 103-16; Pearson and Pryor, *Environment: North and South*; Gladwin and Welles, "Environmental Policy and Multinational Corporate Strategy"; Philip Alston, "International Regulation of Toxic Chemicals," *Ecology Law Quarterly* 7 (1978):397-456; Organization for Economic Cooperation and Development, *State of the Environment in OECD Countries* (Paris: Organization for Economic Cooperation and Development, 1979); Sam Gusman et. al., *Public Policy for Chemicals: National and International Issues* (Washington, D.C.: The Conservation Foundation, 1980); Richard L. Siegel and Leonard B. Weinberg, "Protecting the Environment: Pollution Control Policy," *Comparing Public Policies: United States, Soviet Union and Europe* (Homewood, Ill.: The Dorsey Press, 1977), pp. 378-411; Cynthia Enloe, *The Politics of Pollution in a Comparative Perspective* (New York: David McKay, 1975); and "Cross National Companions in Environmental Protection: A Symposium," *Policy Studies Journal* 11, no. 1 (September 1982):38-175. For recent comparative perspectives on public environmental awareness, see Ronald Inglehart, "Changing Values and the Rise of Environmentalism in Western Societies," *IIES Preprint 14* (Berlin: International Institute for Environment and Society of the Science Center Berlin, 1982); and Hans Kessel, "Comparing Ecological Awareness in Developed Countries," *IIED Preprint 18* (Berlin: International Institute for Environment and Society of the Science Center Berlin, 1982).

8. See Ingo Walter, *Economic Implications of Environmental Policy for Develop-*

ing Countries: Result of an UNCTAD Questionnaire (Geneva: U.N. Commission on Trade and Development, 1976); and Ingo Walter, "Environmental Attitudes in Less Developed Countries," *Resources Policy* 4 (September 1978):200-204 for further discussion.

9. U.S. Department of Commerce, *U.S. Industrial Outlook 1981* (Washington, D.C.: U.S. Government Printing Office, 1981), p. 121.

3. Mineral-Processing Industries

In recent years, the production in the United States of many non-fuel mineral commodities has either declined or grown slowly. Although environmental regulation frequently has come under fire as a main culprit, it has been only one of several forces that have changed the domestic structure of mineral-processing industries and encouraged U.S. companies and foreign producers to process minerals before shipment to the United States.

One important factor is that, throughout the world, both nationalized industries and multinational mining companies are increasingly processing minerals within the country in which they are mined.[1] The governments of nearly all mineral-exporting countries have actively encouraged this trend, even though world processing capacity for most major minerals exceeds mining production. Many governments, concerned more with national prestige and foreign currency receipts than with operating in the black, have subsidized mineral processing by their nationalized industries. Developing countries, especially, have stressed processing minerals within their own borders. They often have been helped in their efforts by international development agencies that have provided advantageous borrowing terms and various forms of technical assistance for processing and refining industries.

Other developments also have contributed to the movement of mineral processors away from the United States. Large increases in transportation costs in recent years have made the processing of minerals at locations closer to mines more attractive, since it is wasteful to transport bulky ores and earthen materials.[2] Meanwhile, U.S. tax laws and other governmental regulations have encouraged, or reduced the risks of, overseas investments by U.S. mineral companies. In addition, numerous nonregulatory economic factors have slowed capital formation in the United States in recent years.

Thus, the main task of this chapter is to outline the extent to which environmental regulations have combined with adverse economic conditions, local processing requirements in various countries, and other factors to reduce the comparative advantage of U.S. producers and to speed the international dispersion of mineral-processing industries. For the purposes of this report, the mineral-processing sector is divided into two main groups—those processing primary and secondary metals and those processing nonmetallic minerals. In each group, key industries that have shown signs of possible "flight" from U.S. environmental regulations (specifically, increased imports, decreased U.S. production, and burdensome regulatory requirements) are examined.

METAL PROCESSORS

The metal-processing industries, which melt and further process ferrous and nonferrous metals, are central to the economies of all industrial societies. Steel and iron in the ferrous grouping and aluminum, copper, lead, zinc, titanium, and nickel in the nonferrous grouping account for more than 80 percent of the production (in dollar value) in the entire sector.[3]

The three dominant industries within the metal sector are steel, iron, and aluminum. The last decade was difficult for all three of these industries, but it does not appear that U.S. processors of these metals have moved significant numbers of their facilities overseas in response to U.S. environmental regulations. To be sure, the U.S. steel industry has declined precipitously as it has been severely undercut by rapidly increasing imports and forced to expend large sums of money on pollution control.[4] This decline has been examined at length by industry analysts, policy makers, and labor groups. Suffice it to say that most observers agree that the causes are many and complex. However, the steel industry is not reexamined here for three reasons:

- Most of the imported steel undercutting U.S. producers has come from government-owned or government-supported steel companies from other nations, not from U.S. companies locating abroad.
- The problems of the U.S. steel industry, virtually every observer concedes, are complex and long-term, not simply due to pollution-control requirements instituted in the 1970s.
- Differences in labor costs among nations are an overwhelming factor in international competition in the steel industry. Between 30 and 40 percent of the cost of steel making is for wages, and U.S. steelworkers earn almost double the wages of their counterparts in Japan and Europe and many times the wages of steelworkers in most newly industrializing nations.[5]

For the iron and aluminum industries, U.S. imports and exports have remained in relative balance in recent years.[6] In addition, both of these industries have special circumstances that are far more important influences on location decisions than are environmental controls—to wit, location of raw materials, energy costs, and transportation costs. For some other key nonferrous metal industries, however, the potential link between increased overseas investment and environmental regulations in the United States is more difficult to track. Traditionally, the United States has been able to satisfy most of its industrial needs for processed nonferrous metals from domestic facilities. Even when domestic deposits of metallic ores were insufficient, ores and concentrates were generally imported and then further processed in this country.

In recent years, this situation has changed rapidly. Decreased investment in new facilities has meant that smelting and refining capacity for most major nonferrous-metal-processing industries has either declined or not kept pace with domestic demand. In addition, both U.S. metal companies and companies representing other nations have markedly increased their overseas primary-metal processing capacities. These increases have occurred in various mineral-rich areas in both developing and developed countries. There has even been an increase in the shipment of ores and concentrates of some metals to intermediate countries for processing before being transported on to the United States and other importing countries.[7]

These trends are expected to continue. A recent report by the General Accounting Office warned that U.S. imports of processed metals, instead of ores and concentrates, will rise during the 1980s.[8] And a 1980 study by the United Nations Industrial Development Organization (UNIDO) noted that select mineral-rich developing countries would process a larger share of the ores mined in their territory in the 1980s than in the 1970s. The UNIDO study also pointed out that plans by some developing countries to establish or expand processing of imported ores would enable developing countries as a whole to process a growing share of world mine production in coming years.[9]

These trends have intensified since new environmental, land-use, and workplace-health regulations were enacted to require fundamental changes in the operations of virtually every metal processor in the United States. Production costs have risen steeply, and an increased percentage of capital has been invested in equipment to reduce waste discharges and improve workplace health and safety. Spending by primary-metal companies on pollution and safety controls averaged nearly 15 percent of total expenditures during the late 1970s.[10] Until 1980, the vast majority of environmental expenditures went toward controlling air and water pollution, but now, as these costs have begun to level off, nonferrous industries have drastically increased spending to comply with new regulations on the treatment, storage, and disposal of hazardous solid wastes. Pollution-control costs went up by more than 30 percent in 1980 from their 1979 level for nonferrous-metal firms.[11] Clearly, by soaking up available capital and dampening the outlook for would-be investors, these steep costs have contributed to the reduction in capacity-creating investments in metal-processing facilities in the United States.

In addition, government and industry reports have argued that metal processors in other developed countries (including Australia, Sweden, West Germany, Ireland, Spain, and Norway) and, much more so, in less-developed countries have been granted more leeway in meeting workplace-health and environmental regulations than have metal processors in the United States.[12] As a result of such concerns, Congress has granted nonferrous smelters exemptions to some sections of the Clean Air Act until 1988 and recently debated proposals to continue the exemptions beyond that time.[13]

Despite all these trends, it is not easy to assess how important environmental regulations have been in the relative decline of domestic metal-processing industries and drastic increases in U.S. imports of most processed metals. What can be said with certainty, however, is that new regulations in recent years have imposed major burdens on nearly every metal-processing industry in the United States. Producers in those industries had already been experiencing increased competition from imports and slow or declining rates of capital investment for new plants and equipment. In some of the specific nonferrous-metal-processing industries discussed below, this extra burden from environmental regulations has affected firms' location decisions and helped create major reductions in domestic processing capacity. In others, the effects of regulatory requirements have been less onerous, because of either the ascendance of other economic factors or the relative ease with which domestic producers have been able to comply with new regulations.

Copper

Historically, the United States has been the world's preeminent miner and processor of copper. It has also been the largest importer and exporter of copper, importing raw concentrates from other copper-mining countries and exporting refined copper and copper products all over the world. While it continues to lead in all phases of basic copper production—mining, ore beneficiation, smelting, refining—the domestic copper industry has experienced many problems that have contributed to a significant erosion in its position vis-à-vis foreign producers during the last two decades. Not least among these problems are the large investments (up to 25 percent of capital spending) that the industry has had to make on pollution-control and workplace-safety equipment to comply with government regulations. In particular, air standards for emissions of sulfur dioxide have had an enormous impact on companies operating copper smelters.

The decline in the relative world status of the U.S. copper industry is unequivocal. In 1964, the United States accounted for 26 percent of the world smelting capacity and 32 percent of the world copper-refining capacity. Large amounts of foreign copper concentrates were imported for smelting and refining, and fully 20 percent of domestic refinery production was exported. By 1974, however, the United States had only 18 percent of the world smelting capacity and 22 percent of refining capacity.[14] In 1980, U.S. smelter capacity was about 16 percent of the world total, and refining had fallen to about 20 percent of world capacity.[15] In addition, the historical pattern whereby the United States imported ores, concentrates, and blister and exported refined copper has been reversed in recent years. Imports of refined copper and exports of unrefined copper have both increased dramatically (figure 3.1).

Actually, until the recent recession, domestic productive capacity for copper smelting and refining, as well as actual production of copper, continued to grow; but it did not expand enough to keep pace with growing domestic demand for copper or with the growth in world output. For example, while U.S. smelting capacity grew only 2 percent between 1964 and 1974, world capacity expanded by 12 percent. Similarly, U.S. copper-refining capacity did not keep pace with the 104 percent increase in world capacity, even though the United States added 29 percent between 1964 and 1974.[16] Nevertheless, by expanding their overseas investments, U.S.-based copper companies have still increased the proportion of world smelting and refining capacity under their control. Unlike their counterparts in the steel industry, U.S. copper producers have been involved in the creation of new smelter and refining capacity abroad. One observer has noted that "the need for major U.S. producers to maintain their world market position by investing in overseas produc-

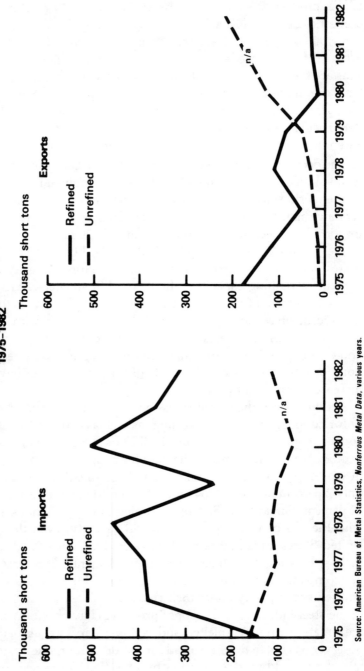

Figure 3.1
U.S. Imports and Exports of Copper,
1975–1982

Source: American Bureau of Metal Statistics, *Nonferrous Metal Data,* various years.

tion has resulted in the relative slippage of the U.S. industry as a factor in world and domestic supply."[17]

All these trends put major pressure on U.S.-based copper producers in the 1970s. Indeed, in 1977-78, imports of refined copper reached such proportions that U.S. producers petitioned the U.S. International Trade Commission (ITC), requesting protection from cheap copper imports. In response, the commission recommended that the president establish import quotas to prevent further injury to the domestic copper industry.[18] President Carter, however, rejected the ITC's recommendation, primarily because of concern that the imposition of copper quotas would undermine efforts to negotiate further trade liberalization at the Tokyo Round talks on the General Agreement on Tariffs and Trade and would significantly increase inflation. In addition, by the time the president acted in 1978 on the copper producers' petition, the short-term pressures of copper imports appeared to be easing.[19]

Extensive studies have been conducted for the domestic copper industry to determine just how significantly it has been hurt by environmental and workplace-health standards. Indeed, probably no other U.S. industry has been the focus of so many such studies. These analyses have identified serious, continuing impacts of the standards and have forecast that existing and proposed regulations will cause domestic copper processing to decline further in the 1980s.[20] The U.S. Bureau of Mines, for example, reported:

> Copper companies continued to make expensive modifications and additions to their smelters in order to comply with required environmental standards—particularly those involving sulfur dioxide and particulate emissions. Several smelters were expected to be closed in the mid-1980s because the capital cost to comply with environmental regulations was not economically justified. In 1978 and 1979 production at a number of smelters was curtailed because of environmental constraints, principally those involving sulfur dioxide emissions.[21]

A study by the U.S. Department of Commerce's Office of Business Policy Analysis predicted in 1979 that compliance with then-existing land-use, pollution-control, and workplace-safety regulations between 1978 and 1987 would require financially strapped firms to invest an additional $1.8 billion. In addition, the report said, those regulations would lead to a no-growth situation for domestic smelting capacity, the probable closing of at least three major smelters, and a price increase of 43 percent above the normally projected price for 1987.[22]

The Commerce Department, noting the increasing export of copper concentrates rather than refined copper, concluded, "Due largely to environmental controls, the current and potential costs to domestic refiners may have provided the incentive to export concentrates rather than install or modify productive capacity."[23]

Several U.S. copper producers echoed these concerns in response to a 1981 Conservation Foundation survey. R. J. Muth, vice-president of Asarco, noted that "copper smelting has been curtailed at existing plants and expansion has been blocked due to EPA SO_2 standards."[24] Similarly, Matthew P. Scanlon, vice-president of Phelps Dodge, said, "Copper concentrates are being shipped from the U.S. for smelting in Japan because EPA [Environmental Protection Agency] and OSHA [Occupational Safety and Health Administration] regulations have forced closure of at least one U.S. smelter and have raised the operating costs of those that remain to the point that they cannot compete with the foreign smelters."[25]

Still, all this concern about the impact of regulations must be put in context. Although there can be no doubt that domestic copper refiners were hit particularly hard by new regulations in the 1970s, it would be a mistake to conclude that this factor alone is responsible for the closure of U.S. smelters, the decreased position of the United States as a producer of smelted and refined copper, and the recent increased shipment of U.S. concentrates abroad. The relative decline of the United States as a producer of refined copper began long before environmental and workplace-health standards became a major drain on capital and operating costs. Between 1960 and 1971, for example, the U.S. share of world refined-copper production dropped from 33 percent to 24 percent.[26] This decline was due primarily to increased output in Japan and the Soviet Union and to the gradually decreasing availability of abundant, easily mined copper deposits in the United States.

Other changes in the structure of the international copper industry also have reduced U.S. dominance. Historically, the world copper industry has been controlled by a small number of highly integrated copper companies from the United States and Western Europe. These companies established claims and opened mines in Australia, Canada, South America, and Africa during the past century. Much of the copper mined in these countries was sent to the developed countries for processing, although smelters were established to produce blister at some of the larger mines in Canada, Australia, Chile, Zaire, and

Zambia. Thus, until recently, except for a small amount of blister, world copper trade was primarily oriented around the flows of ores and concentrates that were mined around the world and then shipped to the United States and Europe for smelting and refining.[27]

Since the early 1960s, however, there have been major changes in these patterns. The opening of newer copper-producing areas (many sending copper to Japan for processing) and the nationalization or partial nationalization of the copper industries of key developing countries has significantly reduced the concentration of ownership and control of world copper production. This has affected U.S. copper producers in at least two significant ways.

First, most mining countries that traditionally have shipped ores and concentrates to the United States have actively sought to increase smelter and refinery capacity to raise the value of their exports. In particular, because there are distinct transportation and other advantages to smelting at or near mining areas, mining countries have substantially increased their smelting capacity, either by creating their own units or by encouraging international firms to do so. Despite these efforts, however, refineries, which are built on a large scale and usually process the blister output of several smelters, remain predominantly located in the developed countries.

Second, with developing countries striving to diversify markets for the raw copper and blister that they still must export, Japanese copper producers have been able to set up long-term agreements for supplies of raw copper and blister to feed their expanding smelting and refinery capacity.[28]

Thus, in many respects, the shifting of the smelting and refining of copper away from the United States has occurred because the time-honored pattern of importing raw copper for processing in the United States was based on a neocolonial relationship between developed and developing countries and a system of oligopolistic control of world copper production by a small number of firms. Neither of these patterns could be maintained, nor will they be duplicated in the future. Moreover, in some cases, U.S. companies apparently contributed to their own problems by being unwilling to adapt to the changing political and economic situations in developing countries. In contrast, Japanese companies, which have not had to bear the burdens of a colonial legacy, have quickly adapted to new modes of doing business with raw-material-supplying countries.[29]

One other set of long-term factors has reduced U.S. copper smelters' ability to compete, especially with Japanese copper smelters, in recent years: shifting locational economics and technological changes within the industry. Environmental regulations, particularly those covering sulfur dioxide, have underlined the significance of these trends, but they have remained secondary variables. Here again, Japanese and, to a lesser extent, European producers have been better situated to take advantage of these changing circumstances.[30]

One major component of this final set of factors is adaptation to changing furnace technologies. Four types of furnaces traditionally have been used for copper smelting: blast, reverberatory, electric, and flash. In the United States, where large-scale copper smelting began about a century ago, the ability of the reverberatory furnace to handle large volumes of concentrate efficiently led to its widespread adoption. The reverberatory process, however, has low thermal efficiency and produces, in the outlet gases, sulfur dioxide in concentrations too low for efficient recovery for market but in volumes so high that they make stack treatment very expensive.[31]

Until recently, neither of these problems significantly affected the U.S. copper industry, since energy was relatively inexpensive and copper smelters were generally located in the American Southwest, far from major population centers. In addition, the isolation of copper smelters from industrial markets in the East and the availability in the United States of sulfur dioxide from low-cost frasch sulfur* have generally made recovering the gas uneconomical for U.S. smelters.

In the past decade, rapid increases in energy costs and growing concern about sulfur dioxide emissions have drastically increased the cost of operating smelters in the United States. However, recovering the gas is still uneconomical for many producers.[32] In contrast, European and Japanese copper smelters widely adopted flash furnace technologies, which produce, as a by-product, a gas well-suited for the commercial manufacture of sulfuric acid. Since the smelters in Europe and Japan commonly have been located near other industrial areas, they have routinely recovered more than 90 percent of the sulfur dioxide produced—and have used it to manufacture sulfuric acid for sale to industrial users.[33] Thus, Japanese and European smelters have been affected less profoundly than U.S. smelters by changing environmental constraints. In fact, Japanese smelters

---

*The frasch process is a method of mining in which very hot water is injected into deep-lying sulfur so that it can be pumped to the surface.

operate not only more efficiently than U.S. smelters but also with much lower fugitive emissions of sulfur dioxide and other flue gases.[34]

Because of their mounting disadvantages, reverberatory furnace smelters are being phased out in the United States and replaced by either flash furnaces, electric furnaces (where large supplies of cheap electricity are available), or newly developed pyrometallurgical (heat-extraction) or hydrometallurgical (liquid-extraction) technologies. However, the poor economic outlook for the past decade, seriously depressed world copper prices through the mid- and late 1970s, and large expenditures for pollution abatement on presently operating facilities have made it difficult for U.S. copper producers to add new smelting capacity quickly enough.[35]

Indeed, the outlook for U.S.-based copper producers is likely to remain seriously depressed through the mid-1980s. The Commerce Department has predicted that domestic shortages of copper could occur by the late 1980s, if the U.S. economy expands rapidly. As has been noted, the federal government has already given copper producers substantial leeway in meeting federal emissions standards in order to ease their fiscal crisis. But industry analysts tend to agree that the two major factors that will determine the future of the U.S. copper industry are the price of copper itself and how quickly U.S. producers adjust to changed production economics—adopting technologies already widely used in Japan and capturing sulfur dioxide within the production process rather than through supplementary control systems.[36] Ironically, any rollback of ambient air-quality standards may simply slow these two changes by reducing the economic disincentives for the U.S. copper producers' present practices.

Zinc

Prior to the late 1960s, the United States was nearly self-sufficient in slab zinc and had the productive capacity to be totally self-sufficient. However, U.S. productive capacity and annual production of the metal dropped rapidly during the early 1970s, while imports were steadily on the rise. Both production and imports fluctuated through the mid-1970s and early 1980s, as a result of market demand. Nevertheless, in every year since 1976 the United States has relied on imports for well over 50 percent of its annual slab zinc consumption (figure 3.2).[37]

The trend toward import dependence paired with a decline of the domestic industry is expected to continue in coming years. The Commerce Department predicted in 1981 that imports would rise from

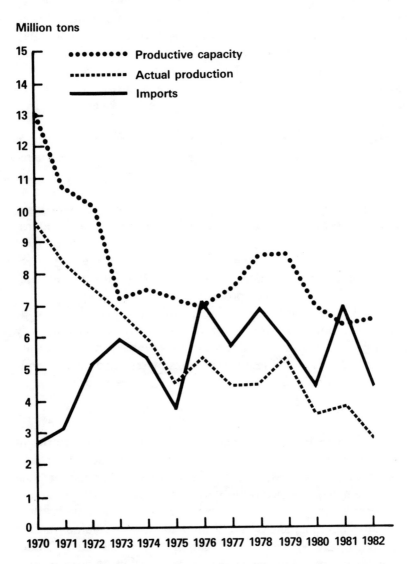

Figure 3.2
U.S. Productive Capacity, Production, and Imports of Slab Zinc, 1970-1982

Million tons

●●●●●●●●● Productive capacity
▪▪▪▪▪▪▪▪▪▪▪▪ Actual production
━━━━━━ Imports

Source: American Metal Market, *Metal Statistics* (New York: Fairchild Publications, various years).

their 51 percent share of the market in 1980 to more than 60 percent of U.S. consumption by the mid-1980s.[38] Although the department forecast that the plant closings and capacity reductions of recent years would level off around 1985, no significant capacity expansions were expected after that, despite continued growth in domestic demand for slab zinc.[39]

Domestic producers often have cited environmental regulations as one of the primary causes of their woes, especially during a rash of shutdowns that occurred in 1979 and 1980. For example, when St. Joe Zinc closed its 250,000-ton-capacity electrothermic zinc smelter at Monaca, Pennsylvania, in December 1979, it claimed that operating the smelter was no longer feasible in light of high energy and manpower requirements and the substantial sums of capital that would be required to meet new environmental regulations.[40] Although this facility has since reopened for partial production, an estimated 200,000 tons of annual domestic capacity have been lost.[41] In addition, New Jersey Zinc, a subsidary of Gulf and Western Industries, recently shut down its Palmerton, Pennsylvania, vertical-retort smelters, reducing capacity by another 118,000 tons.[42]

Still, as with other metal-processing industries, the decline of slab zinc processing in the United States must be examined in the context of long-term factors that have only been intensified by stricter environmental regulations. The 1970s were devastating for the U.S. zinc industry because they marked the confluence of depressed economic conditions, decreasing demand for zinc products, and several factors that had been leading some industry analysts since the end of World War II to predict decreased U.S. zinc production and the closing of many U.S. zinc processors.

Slab zinc can be produced through either pyrometallurgical or hydrometallurgical reduction. There are three types of pyrometallurgical furnaces: horizontal retort, vertical retort, and electrothermic. Hydrometallurgical facilities also are known as electrolytic plants and reduce slab zinc by passing an electrical current through a liquid solution without applying heat.

Horizontal retort furnaces declined rapidly in the United States after World War II because they were dependent upon backbreaking labor operating under conditions of extreme heat, smoke, and fumes. In addition, these furnaces produced only low-grade slab zinc, primarily for galvanizing sheet iron that the military and the construction industry used for protective siding and roofing. When the war was over and the use of less costly substitutes such as asbestos board and aluminum sheet increased, demand for low-purity zinc dropped off rapidly.[43] The last horizontal retort furnaces in the United States closed in 1976.[44]

Vertical retort and electrothermic furnaces are cleaner and can produce a higher grade of slab zinc than horizontal furnaces. However, in recent years they too have operated at a disadvantage to electrolytic smelters, which are even cleaner, are better suited to produce the special high-grade slab that has been in greatest demand, and have much lower labor costs per output. The Palmerton and Monaca, Pennsylvania, plants noted above were the last large pyrometallurgical smelters in the country.[45]

These trends were foreseen long ago by some experts. In 1950, for example, an industry analyst noted that:

> If any conclusions are to be drawn from these facts it must be that the marginal zinc smelters are first, of the horizontal retort type and secondly, in the coal-fuel, high labor cost areas of the Eastern half of the United States. Another indication which may be significant is that new plant capacity being added is predominantly of the electrolytic type.[46]

The same analyst also noted an additional factor that has been integral in the decline of U.S. slab zinc production ever since:

> Another aspect of the zinc industry picture is the recognized fact that the domestic supply of zinc ore is becoming increasingly inadequate to supply the domestic demand for slab zinc. Therefore increasing reliance on foreign ore and/or slab is certain. Evidence of this is borne out statistically by noting that United States imports of zinc in ore for the peak year of 1929 were only 26,000 tons with a domestic mine production of 742,000 tons, as compared with the 1945 data showing imports of 423,000 tons . . ., [thus] domestic to foreign ore being used has diminished from 28:1 in 1929 to the 1945 ratio of about 1.6:1. The competitive position of the domestic smelter is dependent on the tariff policy of the government as well as the consideration of ocean freights, port facilities, rail rates and foreign representatives for his future plans.[47]

U.S.-based companies, operating through their industry trade organization, the Zinc Institute, probably contributed to their own domestic decline by participating in an intensive program to increase consumption of zinc in developing countries during the late 1960s. As part of the program, the Zinc and Lead International Service offered modern technology and marketing support to expand production and consumption in developing countries.[48] Presumably, the assumption was that these countries would supply zinc ore for U.S. producers and purchase more and more processed slab or finished zinc products exported from the United States. Instead, at-home processing has risen rapidly enough in most zinc-mining countries for them to supply growing internal demand and to export slab to the United States.[49]

Meanwhile, in the United States, the slab zinc industry has been experiencing a long-term shrinkage of pyrometallurgical smelter capacity caused by the smelters' reduced competitiveness with electrolytic plants. In addition, the declining availability of U.S. zinc ores, the increased efforts by zinc-mining countries to process ores to slab before export, and a bleak economic situation have all slowed efforts by U.S. producers to replace lost capacity with new electrolytic smelters. The depressed world price of slab zinc during the mid-1970s and a dramatic drop-off in demand for slab as the auto industry searches for lighter substitutes have only exacerbated the problems of U.S. producers. Environmental regulations may have speeded the closing of some vertical retort and electrothermic plants in recent years, but they have not fundamentally affected the long-term factors that are the real causes of the U.S. zinc industry's woes.[50]

Several factors will determine the future of the U.S. industry. Most important, for U.S. zinc producers to recoup, the domestic-demand situation will have to improve enough to warrant investment in new electrolytic plants. This could occur during the late 1980s and early 1990s if various zinc electrical-storage batteries currently being tested are utilized in electrically powered vehicles[51] or if either national security concerns or supply shortages or interruptions lead the federal government to take special steps to aid zinc processors.[52] In addition, a prolonged upturn in the construction industry, as well as new domestic finds of high-grade ores, could significantly improve the outlook for domestic processors.

Lead

Although zinc and lead are often mined together and are both heavily dependent on the auto industry for consumption, their outlooks in the United States differ in several ways. Most important, U.S. mining reserves of high-grade lead that can be recovered economically remain high. Thus, in contrast to zinc and copper, a long-term decline of domestically available lead for processing has not yet set in to squeeze domestic lead smelters and impel their relocation abroad near to raw-material supplies.

Also in contrast to the situations of copper and zinc, the rise to world preeminence of U.S. lead mining and smelting is a relatively recent phenomenon. Not until 1969 did the United States surpass Australia and the Soviet Union to become the world's largest producer of mined lead.[53] Moreover, unlike the U.S. copper industry, U.S. lead smelters have not been directly challenged by Japanese companies, even though Japanese lead smelters have been making rapid strides by relying predominantly on imported raw material. In fact, U.S. exports of primary refined lead have grown in recent years, skyrocketing from 6,000 tons in 1979 to 112,000 tons in 1980 because of high demand for lead in the Japanese and European car industries and by Eastern European countries. Although exports receded to 15,000 tons in 1981, they climbed back up to 49,000 tons in 1982 and an estimated 65,000 tons in 1983; they are expected to remain above their pre-1980 levels for the rest of this decade.[54] During the same time, U.S. imports of primary refined lead are expected to average about 90,000 tons, down considerably from an average of about 240,000 tons in the 1970s (figure 3.3).[55]

Nevertheless, producers of primary refined lead in the United States faced severe problems in the late 1970s as a result of three significant challenges: the continued ascendance of producers of secondary refined lead who utilized scrap lead; weak prices for refined lead; and expanded environmental and workplace-health standards affecting the production and uses of lead and lead products.[56] To date, these adverse circumstances have affected total demand for refined lead more than they have affected the location of primary refined-lead and lead-product manufacturers. Since total demand has been relatively stagnant, there has been no need for U.S. lead consumers to turn to foreign suppliers, nor has there been a strong need for U.S.-based producers to consider lower-cost locations abroad to supply their U.S. markets.

The lead industry—both primary and secondary producers— fought both EPA's national ambient air-quality standard established for lead in 1978 and OSHA standards on occupational exposure to lead, claiming that they could force all lead plants to close because the industry lacked the technology to comply.[57] However, because these standards have not been fully implemented, they have not resulted directly in major capacity reductions for U.S. lead producers.

Rather, the most significant effects of environmental and related standards on U.S. lead production have come on the demand side.[58] About 65 percent of all lead consumed in the United States is used

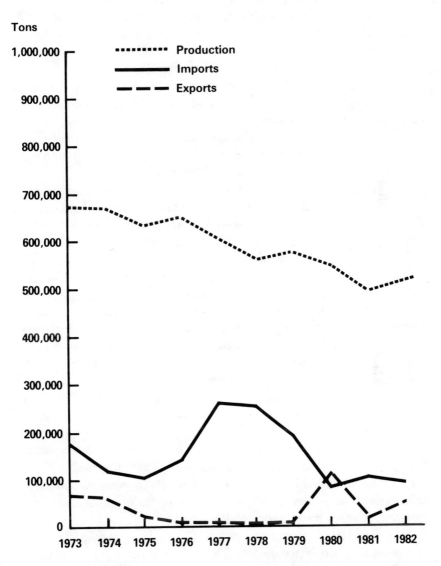

Figure 3.3
U.S. Production, Imports, and Exports
of Primary Refined Lead, 1973–1982

Source: U.S. Bureau of Mines, *Minerals Yearbook*, "Lead," (Washington, D.C.: U.S. Department of Interior, various years).

for batteries. The prolonged downturn in U.S. automobile sales has thus been a major factor in the weak demand for lead. Conversely, the surge of foreign-made autos has been partly responsible for increased export of lead refined in the United States for use in batteries in foreign cars. The second largest demand for lead is as an antiknock additive for gasoline (tetraethyl lead). However, restrictions on the use of leaded gasoline have caused continuous declines in lead demand for this use. Impending EPA efforts to eliminate all leaded gasoline will only further reduce demand in the future. The other major use for lead—in pigments and paints—also has continued to decline as new safety standards have reduced the amount of lead these products can contain.[59]

Ironically, though, the declining demand for lead has tended to cause more problems for secondary producers of scrap lead than for primary producers of smelted lead. Primary producers produced an annual average of about 600 short tons per production facility between 1977 and 1982 and operated their plants at near-full capacity. By contrast, per-facility secondary production fell from 830 short tons in 1977 to 600 short tons by 1982, and producers in 1982 utilized only about 55 percent of their productive capacity.[60]

The real challenge for domestic lead producers probably is still to come. To date, environmental and related regulations, in tandem with the depressed economic situation, have affected lead production primarily by causing declines in demand, which have then caused producers to hold back production. The Commerce Department predicts that the combination of poor economic return, existing EPA and OSHA standards, and potential new regulations (the Clean Water Act requires EPA to set standards for water-borne lead by 1984) could lead to a reduction in U.S. lead-production capacity over the next three to five years.[61] If the automobile economy picks up suddenly, or some new market application rapidly increases demand for lead, it could provoke domestic shortages of lead during the 1980s. In the long term, increased imports of lead products (especially batteries) could result, as foreign producers gain potential markets and U.S.-based producers move more of their capacity abroad.[62]

So for lead producers, environmental and related regulations have really been a two-edged sword. Thus far, the most significant impact has been demand-related, but, in the future, U.S. production capacity may also decline as some producers close plants because they lack the technology to meet standards or cannot generate the capital to install control equipment.

Still, although the effects of present and forthcoming regulations on lead producers should be carefully monitored, it appears that, in the long term, the outlook for the U.S. lead industry will hinge fundamentally on demand. If new applications for the metal replace declining use in gasoline and pigments, and if battery production surges, it is likely that the rising price and profit potential will induce producers to create new capacity and to equip existing capacity to meet environmental standards.[63] The fact that the majority of the world's known minable lead is in the United States makes it unlikely that large-scale lead and lead-product manufacturing for the U.S. market will take place abroad in times of extended good economic outlook.

Arsenic Trioxide

Arsenic is present as an impurity in ores that are processed for their content of nonferrous metals, especially copper, zinc, lead, gold, and silver. Most ores do not contain high enough levels of arsenic to warrant recovery, however, so many smelting operations emit arsenic as an unwanted, unrecovered by-product.

Since arsenic is highly toxic and poses significant hazards to humans and animals, new regulations have sought to reduce substantially the amounts of arsenic released into the air and water by smelting operations. Efforts to eliminate by-product arsenic from smelter stack gases and flue dusts have posed financial and logistical hardships for many smelters, particularly those producing copper.[64]

Some by-product arsenic is recovered commercially for use in chemical and related industries. Although arsenic can be recovered in its metallic (and less toxic) form, the demand for metallic arsenic is extremely limited. Instead, most arsenic is recovered and marketed in its trioxide form.[65] Arsenic trioxide, or white arsenic, is used primarily in the formulation of arsenical pesticide compounds, as a decolorizer and refining agent in the manufacture of glass, in the production of wood preservatives, and in the preparation of pharmaceutical products.[66] Demand for arsenic has not increased very much in recent years and is expected to climb by no more than 1 percent per year during the 1980s, in part because of concerns about the health and safety of workers in factories using arsenical compounds and about the toxicity of arsenical products.[67]

Only smelters specially equipped to process ores with high arsenic content can recover arsenic trioxide commercially. The procedures for doing so are complicated, prone to malfunctioning, inefficient, and unable to totally stop the escape of waste arsenic. As a result, only a few producers of arsenic trioxide exist in the world, including a copper smelter in Tacoma, Washington, operated by Asarco, and since 1965 the only U.S. producer of arsenic trioxide.[68]

Imports have long accounted for a substantial portion of U.S. consumption of arsenic trioxide. Between 1955 and 1959, the share of imports rose from about 35 percent of U.S. consumption to about 65 percent.[69] U.S. consumption and production figures have not been officially reported since 1959 (to avoid disclosing confidential data of individual companies), but imports apparently rose again in 1967 and 1968 to almost 80 percent of the domestic consumption. In both 1959 and 1967-68, the increases in imports were largely due to strikes that were hitting the domestic copper industry. During 1967-68, for example, Asarco's copper smelter at Tacoma, Washington, operated on a sharply curtailed production schedule because of a lengthy strike.[70] After 1968, imports receded to previous levels and Asarco's production remained at that level through 1973, with the exception of 1971, when another strike brought production down to 7,500 short tons. However, imports did not increase in 1971, because U.S. domestic stocks were sufficient to cover the shortfall.[71]

Between 1973 and the early 1980s, U.S. and world production and importation patterns for arsenic trioxide shifted markedly (figure 3.4). First, U.S. production tapered off, dropping by more than 50 percent between 1973 and 1977. Second, U.S. imports declined sharply in 1976, but climbed once again after that. Third, Sweden, long the largest foreign supplier of arsenic trioxide for the United States, lost that position to Mexico and France for several years, but by 1979 had regained its predominance. Fourth, during the middle and late 1970s, even while total world production fell, processing increased in several industrializing countries, notably Mexico and Peru, and ambitious plans for arsenic trioxide production were made in the Philippines. Fifth, worldwide production of arsenic trioxide declined about 20 percent from the average production of the 1960s; as a result, worldwide demand for arsenic trioxide, although itself relatively stable, exceeded supply in both 1978 and 1979, and manufacturers in the United States, Sweden, and Mexico were forced to ration supplies to customers.

Because arsenic trioxide is produced as a by-product of the smelting of major metallic ores, fluctuations in its production are usually best

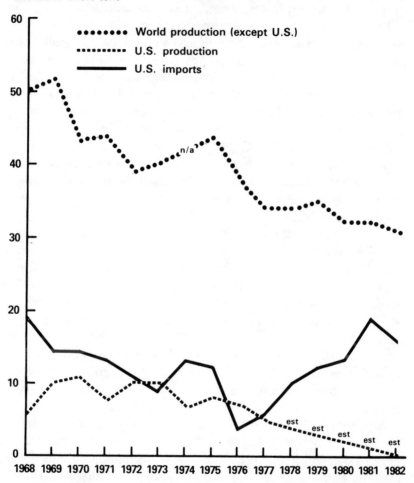

**Figure 3.4
World Production, U.S. Production,
and U.S. Imports of Arsenic Trioxide,
1968-1982**

Thousand short tons

•••••••• World production (except U.S.)
---------- U.S. production
—— U.S. imports

U.S. production data after 1977 were withheld by manufacturers to avoid disclosing proprietary information.

Source: William A. Vogely, ed., *Economics of the Metal Industries*, 3rd ed. New York: American Institute of Mining, Metallurgical and Petroleum Engineers, 1976), p. 825; Stanford Research Institute, "Arsenic Trioxide," in *Chemical Economics Handbook* (Menlo Park, Calif.: Stanford Research Institute, 1979), p. 710.2000C; U.S. Bureau of the Census, *U.S. Imports for Consumption and General Imports*, FT246, annual editions, 1974–79, TSUSA No.4176200; "Minor Metals," in *Minerals Yearbook 1978–79* (Washington, D.C.: U.S. Bureau of Mines, 1980), p. 1036; and *Mineral Commodity Summaries 1983* (Washington, D.C.: U.S. Bureau of Mines, 1983).

explained by factors affecting production of those major metals.* None of these five trends, however, can be explained adequately by factors affecting production of arsenic's coproducts. Instead, all of the trends directly correlate with environmental regulatory initiatives and public concern in the United States and abroad.

In 1974, the first year of sliding U.S. production, OSHA took its first steps to initiate new minimum-exposure standards for allowable arsenic concentrations in the workplace, proposing that they be reduced to "no detectable level." During the same period, studies appeared showing that very high rates of death from cancer existed among Tacoma smelter workers and that children living within a half-mile of the smelter had absorbed as much arsenic as the workers themselves had. Although OSHA eventually settled for a 10-milligram arsenic standard and permitted a gradual movement toward it, environmental restrictions were, without question, the primary factor limiting production of arsenic products between 1974 and 1980, as the Bureau of Mines concluded.[73]

Indeed, even while its overall copper output has remained relatively stable in recent years, Asarco has been terminating agreements to accept arsenic residues from other smelters and to process high-arsenic copper ores that it imported in large amounts during the early 1970s. Apparently, the major remaining source of arsenic now produced at Tacoma is arsenical residue from Asarco's own lead smelter in Montana.[74]

Asarco's reduction in imports of high-arsenic ores and its overall reduction in arsenic trioxide produced have had direct impacts in three industrializing countries in particular. In Peru, which had once been a major supplier of high-arsenic ores for the Takoma plant, Asarco's partially owned subsidiary nearly doubled production of arsenic trioxide between 1976 and 1979; exports to the United States of refined arsenic trioxide averaged nearly 1 million pounds during the mid- and late 1970s. Similarly, Asarco's partially owned Mexican subsidiary has also stepped up production of arsenic trioxide, although imports to the United States have fluctuated.[75] Finally,

---

*As noted, the 1959, 1967-68, and 1971 dips in U.S. arsenic trioxide production all coincided with reduced copper smelting caused by labor strife. Another example of arsenic trioxide's relationship to other metals' production occurred between 1976 and 1979, when low world prices and waning high-grade ores prompted Tsumeb Corporation, the only Namibian producer of arsenic trioxide, to curtail its production of lead.[72]

Lepanto Consolidated Ltd., a Philippines company, has constructed an 18,000-metric-ton per year copper-concentrate roasting plant to accommodate high-arsenic concentrates that it once sent to Asarco's Tacoma plant.[76]

Fluctuations in production of arsenic trioxide at the copper smelter in Sweden and reduced exports to the United States in the mid-1970s both seem attributable to Swedish environmental concern and regulations. As in the United States, workplace and pollution regulations governing the release of arsenic were made much more stringent in Sweden during those years. In the long run, with the Tacoma smelter slated for shutdown, the United States is likely to remain heavily dependent on imported arsenic trioxide from Mexico, Sweden, France, and the Philippines.

NONMETALLIC-MINERAL PRODUCERS

The nonmetallic-mineral industries produce a wide range of materials that are generally used in bulk amounts in building materials and chemical products. This basic grouping includes asbestos, cement, clays, gypsum, gravel, stone, sand, and several chemical minerals such as potash, phosphate, and sulfur. Unlike metals, nonmetallic minerals are not processed by smelting. Rather, they are generally crushed, filtered, washed, or otherwise separated prior to reconstitution with other materials. As a consequence, the two major environmental problems in these industries have tended to be those related to the dust or fibers that escape in bulk processing and to the large amounts of waste muds that often are left over.

Usually, the most important factor in choosing sites for facilities to process and formulate nonmetallic minerals has been, not pollution and workplace-safety concern, but proximity to the source of the raw material—a quarry or mine. There is some indication, however, that increased environmental regulation has been a factor in decreased U.S. production and increased U.S. imports for two widely used nonmetallic-mineral commodities: asbestos and cement.

Asbestos

Asbestos is really the generic name for the fibrous varieties of several minerals. Although these asbestos minerals differ in chemical composition, as a group they share several unique and commercially desirable properties that vary according to the length, diameter, strength, and flexibility of the fibers. The most significant of these properties are resistances to heat, flame, chemicals, moisture, abrasion, and corrosion. Asbestos minerals also can be individually fiberized and processed in a similar fashion to natural fibers such as wool, silk, and cotton. As a result, in most of their nearly 3,000 uses, asbestos fibers are mixed with numerous other substances to provide insulation from fire, heat, electricity, and chemicals; to increase the strength of many composition materials (cement, paper, plastics, asphalt, coatings, resins, and filling compounds); and to reduce wear due to friction. There are few good substitutes for asbestos; for many commercial uses, asbestos is easily the best material from the standpoints of performance, economic cost, and availability.[77]

However, because asbestos's light, flexible fibers are easily airborne, they are inhaled or ingested into the bodies of those who work around the mineral or who use asbestos-containing products where the fibers can be freed from their containing medium. When inhaled, most asbestos fibers pass through the gastrointestinal tract and out of the body, but some remain in the lungs and other parts of the body. It has long been known that prolonged exposure to asbestos dust can lead to a chronic, debilitating, dust-related lung disease known as asbestosis. But concern about asbestos has become much more widespread with the publication of evidence that exposure at levels far below those that induce asbestosis can cause lung cancer and mesothelioma (an otherwise rare, untreatable cancer of the chest and stomach lining). Evidence has now accumulated linking asbestos to cancers contracted by people who have had little or no direct contact with asbestos products: people who have lived in towns where a production facility used asbestos; family members who have been exposed only to the fiber dust carried home on work clothes; adults who as children were exposed to asbestos tailings for brief periods or who played with toys cut from asbestos clapboard.[78]

Because of these findings, asbestos was one of the first three substances to be labeled as a hazardous air pollutant under the Clean Air Act and was the first hazardous substance regulated when OSHA was created. Since then, the asbestos industry has been fundamentally altered by a deluge of regulations governing workplace health and environmental pollution, including standards and restrictions set by OSHA to cover workplace exposure, by EPA to regulate fiber emissions into the air and water and onto the land, and by the Consumer Product Safety Commission to reduce public exposure to asbestos when products manufactured with asbestos fibers are used.[79]

But at least as important as the direct regulatory assaults on asbestos have been the massive fiscal problems associated with growing public and worker awareness of the serious long-term health problems that exposure to asbestos can cause. Foremost among these problems are the large legal costs and potential judgments (running into the billions of dollars) forced upon asbestos producers by the thousands of lawsuits filed against them on behalf of individuals who have contracted diseases linked with asbestos.[80] In addition, public concern about asbestos has become so widespread that its producers and users have had to embark on major spending campaigns to remove, replace, and find substitutes for the mineral in hundreds of its applications.[81]

As a result, asbestos use in several consumer products in the United States has diminished or been eliminated altogether. In particular, asbestos-containing products (for example, fire logs, filtering aids, paving materials, and spackling and joint cement) that can be mishandled or whose use involves direct contact with free fibers by the public have been removed from the market.[82] The use of asbestos shingles and clapboard has declined markedly with the introduction of safer, less expensive, and more durable materials. Demand for asbestos cement has also declined, primarily because the need for new municipal waterworks, sewage networks, irrigation projects, and low-cost industrial and residential buildings has lessened as the economy has matured.[83] Finally, nonasbestos thermal-insulation products have been widely marketed, using such substitutes as fiberglass, steel wool, slag wool, and ceramic materials.[84]

Nevertheless, asbestos remains, and likely will remain, a widely used industrial material in the United States. Despite strong pressures to find them, satisfactory substitutes still do not exist for many uses of asbestos, particularly applications where the quality of the end product depends on the tensile strength of asbestos. For example, viable substitutes have been slow to come on the market for use in many frictional products, textiles, coating and paint compounds, paper products, and gaskets and packing materials made from asbestos.[85] Thus, overall consumption of asbestos has been relatively stable in the United States. Indeed, total domestic demand for asbestos products is expected to increase moderately until at least the year 2000, providing major end uses are not banned outright before then.[86]

The fact that domestic demand for some asbestos-containing end-use products remains strong despite the difficulties in overcoming problems of exposure during production has significant implications for location decisions within the asbestos industry. The industry clearly is experiencing substantial pressure to process and manufacture products abroad. In fact, producers in some segments of the asbestos industry have long contended that new U.S. regulations encourage a strategy of locating production activities overseas. For example, a vice-president for Johns-Manville Corporation testified in 1972 that adoption of a proposed standard for asbestos in the workplace would "cause a significant number of jobs to be shifted to foreign workers." He added, "We would simply be shifting the problem to other workers in the world, solely because of unrealistic and unnecessary regulations."[87]

It is difficult to assess whether this predicted transfer of facilities has occurred on an industry-wide basis. Data on total imports of asbestos-containing products are hard to accumulate because asbestos is used in such a wide variety of manufactured goods. Figures on garments, textiles, vinyl floorings, and other finished products that contain asbestos often cannot be separated from figures for asbestos-free imports of the same goods. The Commerce Department does, however, keep separate statistics for two categories of intermediate asbestos-containing products—asbestos yarns and asbestos pipes. U.S. imports of those two goods have have actually declined from their high levels in the mid-1970s (figures 3.5 and 3.6). This appears to reflect declining U.S. demand for the products, as asbestos-free substitutes have been used.

Despite such declines, there are signs that some segments of the U.S. asbestos industry have pursued a strategy of relocation. It is interesting to note, for example, that Mexico and Taiwan have recently replaced Canada and the United Kingdom as the principal suppliers of asbestos yarns to the United States. Conversely, Canadian sales of asbestos pipes to the United States have experienced a resurgence in recent years after a hiatus in the 1970s, during which Mexico was the largest source of U.S. imports. These trends suggest that Canadian producers—with the world's largest reserves of unmined asbestos and intricate ties with U.S. firms—are using more of their raw asbestos to produce pipes than to produce yarns, textiles, and garments. In contrast, Mexican producers with close ties to producers and marketers in the United States may have chosen to concentrate more on asbestos yarns and textile products, as many recent studies of *maquiladora* (or border-zone plant) operations also suggest.[88] The Mexican government appears to have encouraged the buildup of light manufacturing industries using asbestos in the border region at the same time that manufacturing plants in the United States have been subjected to intense public and governmental scrutiny.[89]*

At the same time, not all segments of the industry have sought to relocate. Wide variations can be found in the impacts that environmental regulations, litigation, and public concern have had on the location decisions of domestic producers. These variations tend to be influenced most heavily by the degree to which dangers from asbestos exposure arise within the workplace, in the local environment, in product use, or in waste disposal following consumption of the product.

In general, the strongest pressures for relocating asbestos-manufacturing facilities overseas will be on the segments of the industry—such as those making textiles, pipes, and brake shoes—that share several characteristics:

- The elasticity of demand for the use of asbestos in the particular product remains low—that is, substitutes are inferior, expensive, or unavailable.
- Production tends to be labor-intensive and difficult to automate.
- The main problem of exposure is concentrated within a limited area and population (for example, workers in the factory) and is difficult to alleviate with production-process technology.
- The dangers of exposure from further manufacturing or consumption of the imported asbestos products are reduced because the asbestos fibers in the final product are "incarcerated," meaning

---

*There are indications that the Mexican government no longer views the transfer of labor-intensive, low-technology asbestos-related production from the United States to Mexico as a desirable trend. Thus, Manuel Medellin Milan, then the director for the chemical industry in the Ministry of National Patrimony and Industrial Development, said in 1982 that the ministry had recently rejected a proposal from a U.S. company to build a new plant to produce asbestos products in Mexico:

We did not accept the company's motives for wanting to come to Mexico. We think the problems of asbestos have been exaggerated in the United States, but we do not want to get involved with a company if it is running away from those problems. We are prepared to live with the risks associated with asbestos if it is for our own domestic needs, but we will not accept asbestos companies anymore if they want solely to produce for export.[90]

Another indication that U.S. producers may find it increasingly difficult to flee U.S. regulations by opening plants overseas comes from the fate of a Raybestos Manhattan brake-pad facility built in Ireland during the mid-1970s. When Irish workers and local citizens later learned of the perils of asbestos, they initiated a series of protests and legal actions that culminated in late 1980 with the closing of the plant.[91]

68

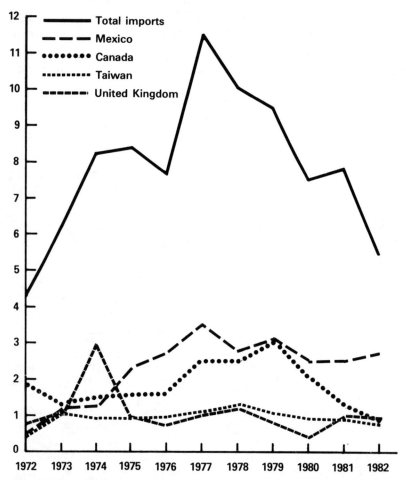

**Figure 3.5
U.S. Imports of Asbestos Yarns,
Silvers, etc.,
by Country of Origin, 1972–1982**

Million pounds

Legend:
——— Total imports
— — — Mexico
•••••••• Canada
············ Taiwan
-------- United Kingdom

Source: U.S. Bureau of the Census, *U.S. Imports for Consumption and General Imports*, FT 246, annual editions.

Figure 3.6
U.S. Imports of Asbestos Pipes,
Tubes, and Fittings,
by Country of Origin, 1972-1982

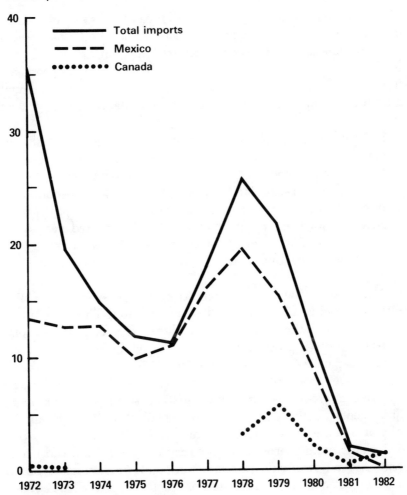

Million pounds

Canadian data not available for 1974–1977.

Source: See figure 3.5.

that the products can be more-or-less safely imported into the United States while the side effects are felt in the producing country.

Cement

Hydraulic cements are dry powders that can bind sand and gravel into concrete. Because cement is indispensable to all major forms of construction activity—commercial, residential, industrial, and public works—it is one of the most widely used mineral products. In fact, among all nonfuel minerals, only iron, steel, and aluminum are produced in higher quantities and consume more energy than cement.[92]

Historically, the U.S. cement industry has been led by small- and medium-sized producers serving regional markets. This is because cement, with a low value-to-weight ratio, is expensive to transport over land; a general rule in the past was that it was uneconomical to transport cement more than 200 miles over land. This has changed somewhat, however, for production facilities located near water transportation. The advent of large container ships for cement has made it more economical to transport cement long distances by water.[93]

After World War II, supply and demand for cement were fairly well balanced in all regions of the United States. Then, rapid construction during the building booms of the 1950s led to large expansions of domestic productive capacity during the decade. U.S. productive capacity apparently peaked in 1967, when 188 plants could produce well over 100 million short tons annually. After that, the overall U.S. productive capacity began to fall steadily, despite average annual consumption increases of over 3 percent. By 1971 the number of plants in the United States had dropped to 180, and in 1977 only 157 plants, with a productive capacity of 92.6 million short tons, remained in operation. The number of plants operating in 1982 was 152, with about an 89-million-ton productive capacity.[94] As a result of this decline, spot shortages arose during the 1970s and have recurred periodically in regions experiencing rapid growth and construction: the Southeast, especially Florida; the West Coast; the Southwest; and certain areas of the Midwest.[95]

During the 1970s, large quantities of cement frequently were imported to make up for these shortfalls in domestic production. Thus, during 1973, when Florida and other southeastern states were in the middle of a building boom, producers of cement relied on imports to meet their commitments, and several large users of cement imported cement directly from foreign producers.[96] Similarly, in the summer and fall of 1978, regional shortages in California and the Southwest led to a marked increase in cement imports from Japan.[97] Overall, U.S. dependence on imports rose significantly during the 1970s, with imports averaging about 10 percent of total consumption by the end of the decade.[98]

The makeup of U.S. imports of hydraulic cement also changed dramatically during this time. For example, clinker (a mixture of calcareous rock, silica, alumina, and iron oxide that has already been clumped together in a hot kiln) became much more important as a percentage of total U.S. cement imports. During the 1960s, clinker accounted for less than 10 percent of total cement imports. This figure rose to 15 percent in 1970 and to 24 percent in 1971. In 1972, clinker passed the 30 percent mark, and in 1979 it accounted for just under 50 percent of U.S. cement imports (figure 3.7).[99]

Increased environmental regulations undoubtedly have contributed to the domestic plant closings, the increased imports of hydraulic cement, and the shift to importing greater quantities of clinker. A report during the late 1970s by the Bureau of Mines noted:

> Clinker grinding facilities were becoming increasingly important as quasi-cement production units. Also, several large plants supplemented clinker production with imported clinker. Rather than comply with air pollution regulations, some companies have shut down kilns but continue to operate grinding mills on imported clinker.[100]

The main pollutants in the manufacture of cement are fine dust particles from the plant stacks and water-borne alkalies that are leached from the cement. These pollutants are primarily generated during the production of clinker, especially from the kiln and the clinker cooler associated with the kiln. Thus, by shifting from in-house production of clinker to use of clinker purchased abroad or from other domestic producers, some U.S. firms have been able to avoid large expenditures for electrostatic precipitators or fabric-bag dust collectors to reduce pollution.[101]

However, it appears that this is neither a satisfactory long-term strategy for U.S. producers nor the dominant strategy being pursued by the most dynamic and growing firms within the U.S. cement industry. Rather, this response appears most prevalent among two types of firms: (*a*) those operating small, outmoded cement-

Figure 3.7
U.S. Imports of Cement and Clinker,
1970-1981

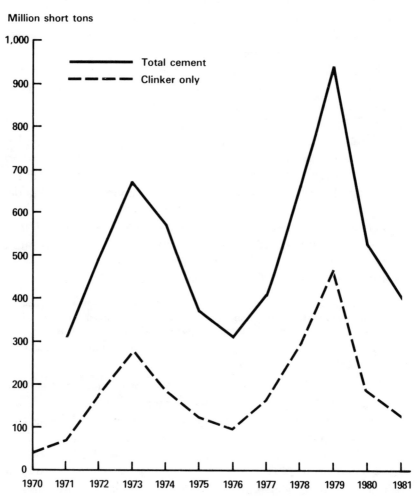

Million short tons

Source: U.S Bureau of the Census, *U.S. Imports for Consumption and General Imports*, FT246, annual editions, TSUSA Nos.5111420, 5111440.

production facilities, and (b) those that for various reasons have not invested heavily in new production facilities and upgraded technology in recent years and instead have sought to diversify into new product areas or invest overseas to secure future profits. The market share of both types of firms has declined in recent years, as rapid changes have occurred in the economies of scale for the production of cement and in the makeup of the companies that dominate the industry. As a result, increases in cement imports, and in particular clinker imports, can only be viewed in the context of fundamental long-term economic trends in U.S. cement production and the reactions to those trends by different types of firms within the industry.

Because of their plant-building spree during the 1950s, many cement producers found themselves with adequate, or even surplus, productive capacity during the 1960s and in the early 1970s. However, not long after these plants were built, technological advances, as well as fiscal pressures to save on unit labor costs and reduce energy consumption, made many of them obsolete. Moreover, many of those plants had very limited productive capacities and were either the sole production facility or one of only two such facilities owned by their company. In 1950, the average cement-plant capacity was 1.78 million barrels per annum, and even in 1960 only a handful of plants could produce 3 million barrels of cement annually.[102] A 1972 study of the industry by the Boston Consulting Group pointed out:

> In general, the profitability of a cement plant is a function of its age and size, and its share of the regional market in which it is located. Naturally plants in sparsely populated areas are smaller than those near major metropolitan markets. The plants in the weakest comparative position today are generally those of under three million consumption area.[103]

Despite the changed economic situation within the industry, many traditional cement-producing firms were unable or unwilling to respond by building larger production facilities during the late 1960s and early 1970s. Small firms simply continued to operate marginal facilities because many of those plants still had not paid for themselves and the firms could not raise the capital to invest in larger-scale facilities. Environmental-control costs, necessitated during the late 1960s and the 1970s, certainly sped the trend to close these inefficient production units, but obsolescence due to small size was the real reason for the demise of many cement-production units.[104] By 1970 the average plant capacity in the cement industry had risen to 2.86 million barrels, and in 1980 the average facility could produce over 3 million barrels.[105]

During the late 1960s and the 1970s, many of the larger cement firms that had dominated the industry in the early postwar years, and that were in a better position than the small firms to invest in new large-scale production facilities, also did not do so. With profits in the industry experiencing a cyclical decline during the early 1970s, and with the industry further squeezed by the need to make large expenditures on pollution equipment and the rising price of energy, many of the traditional industry leaders were reluctant to invest in new capacity. Instead, a 1978 Bureau of Mines report said:

> Some companies have invested in foreign cement manufacturing ventures with anticipated higher returns, while others have diversified into a wide range of enterprises, including the floor-covering industry, furniture industry, real estate development, recreational land development, leisure time products, building materials sales, general construction, and potash production for fertilizers.[106]

Not all producers of cement have shared this conservative domestic outlook, however. Several new firms have rapidly expanded their capacity in new large plants in recent years and increased their overall market shares. Inevitably, the market share of the older leading companies has declined: in 1978, for example, only 1 of the top 10 cement-producing companies in the United States had been among the top 8 producers in 1950. The newcomers that now dominate the field of the largest cement producers in the United States include large ready-mix concrete firms that have integrated backwards into cement; gypsum and other building-products manufacturers; new companies organized by mineral and mining companies; and foreign cement companies that have been investing heavily in the U.S. market.[107] Unlike a number of traditional cement companies, many of these newcomers have been realizing substantial profits and building new facilities at a healthy rate in the United States. During 1978 and 1979, for example, at least 14 new or remodeled cement plants opened in the United States; all of them utilized the modern dry-process kiln and were equipped to produce more than three million barrels of cement per year. Numerous new plants, expansions, and modernizations were also planned for the early 1980s. With few exceptions, these new facilities seemingly have had little difficulty in meeting current pollution-control standards.[108]

In light of the dual structure of innovative, new producers and traditional, older ones that has emerged in the cement industry in recent years, it appears that many of the plant closings and much of the growth in overall import dependence and in imports of clinker can be attributed to declining companies within the industry. Small companies have simply found it difficult to make ends meet; many have folded or sold out to larger producers. Larger firms that once dominated the industry have declined, moved into new product lines, or been bought up by foreign companies or other U.S. companies. During this state of flux, cement shortages have necessitated higher imports. Environmental regulations have increased the velocity of these trends but have been only peripherally responsible for them.

As figure 3.7 shows, imports of concrete and clinker have receded from their late 1970s levels. However, in the near future, at least, it is unlikely that they will fall back much further to their previous low levels, since cement imports are far more economical than they were before the 1970s. The bulk of current U.S. cement imports come from Canada or from countries with surplus capacities of their own and production facilities located near deepwater ports for shipment to coastal markets. In addition, in the 1970s, the General Agreement on Tariffs and Trade substantially reduced tariffs on imported cement and clinker.[109]

Despite the fact that imports will likely remain high, environmental regulations are not likely to necessitate the closing of any profitable cement-production facilities in the future, nor are they likely to inhibit new expansions during the late 1980s. The newer, larger and technologically advanced cement facilties that are being built in the 1980s appear to be having far fewer environmental difficulties than most of those facilities that were shuttered in the 1970s had. However, it is likely that the poor economic outlook and the enforcement of pollution standards will continue to speed the demise of remaining small facilities.

CONCLUSIONS

In most cases, environmental regulations have not directly caused whatever exodus of mineral-processing companies from the United States has occurred. There does, however, appear to be evidence to corroborate a recent World Bank study. That study postulated that a preliminary reaction to rigorous environmental regulations by international firms headquartered in countries belonging to the Organization for Economic Cooperation and Development has been to look more seriously at the prospects of relocating processing facilities in developing countries. But, the study concluded, after the initial uncertainty and disruptive effects caused by the regulations, those regulations have had—and will continue to have—little effect on the worldwide distribution of mineral-processing capacity.[110]

This seems to be the case in the United States. During the initial period of increased environmental regulations, many U.S. mineral-processing facilities experienced hardships, and marginal plants closed. In some cases, new plants were built abroad to compensate. These trends were reinforced by several other adverse circumstances faced in the 1970s by U.S. mineral processors. In the long run, however, the health of three key mineral-processing industries in the United States—copper, zinc, and cement—will depend more on economic trends, technological innovation, and the availability of quality raw materials in the United States than on environmental regulations.

Two mineral-processing industries—asbestos and arsenic trioxide —do appear to have been forced into more overseas production as a direct result of environmental regulations in the United States. But domestic consumption of many asbestos products and arsenic trioxide is expected to continue to fall in coming years, so it does not seem likely that new production capacity would be opened in the United States even if standards were relaxed.

The case of lead is complex, since environmental and health hazards associated with the metal have caused domestic demand for lead products to decline even more rapidly than U.S. production. If U.S. demand for lead were to increase rapidly (owing, perhaps, to a widespread introduction of electric cars), a combination of environmental, workplace-health, and economic constraints might prevent U.S. lead producers from expanding domestic production quickly enough. In such a case, many of those producers might relocate overseas, increasing U.S. dependence on imported lead.

REFERENCES

1. See United Nations Industrial Development Organization (UNIDO), *Mineral Processing in Developing Countries* (New York: United Nations, 1977); Rex Bossan and Bension Varon, *The Mining Industry and the Developing Countries* (London: Oxford University Press, 1977); and Georgia Sambunaris, "Strategic Minerals and the Third World," *AID Agenda*, July-August 1981.

2. UNIDO, *Mineral Processing in Developing Countries*; Bossan and Varon, *The Mining Industry and the Developing Countries*; and Sambunaris, "Strategic Minerals and the Third World."

3. U.S. Department of Commerce, *U.S. Industrial Outlook 1981* (Washington, D.C.: U.S. Government Printing Office, 1981), pp. 191-93.

4. U.S. Department of Commerce, *U.S. Industrial Outlook 1983* (Washington, D.C.: U.S. Government Printing Office, 1983), p. 18-3.

5. For two different perspectives, see Robert W. Crandall, *The U.S. Steel Industry in Recurrent Crisis* (Washington, D.C.: Brookings Institution, 1981); and *Steel at the Crossroads: One Year Later, A Progress Report on the American Steel Industry* (Washington, D.C.: American Iron and Steel Institute, 1981).

6. U.S. Department of Commerce, *U.S. Industrial Outlook 1983*, pp. 18-5, 19-10.

7. U.S. Department of Commerce, *U.S. Industrial Outlook 1981*, pp. 191-99.

8. Cited in Ibid., p. 194.

9. UNIDO, *Mineral Processing in Developing Countries*, p. 73.

10. U.S. Department of Commerce, *U.S. Industrial Outlook 1981*, p. 196.

11. Ibid.

12. See, especially, "The U.S. Mining and Mineral-Processing Industry: An Analysis of Trends and Implications" (Report to the Congress of the United States by the Comptroller General of the United States), October 31, 1979, pp. 26-28, 41-42. For more balanced perspectives, see T. K. Corwin et al., *International Technology for the Nonferrous Smelting Industry* (Park Ridge, N.J.: Noyes Data Corp., 1982), and J. Larsen, "Comparative Philosophy of Environmental Regulations," in *Sulfur Dioxide Control in Pyrometallurgy* (Proceedings of conference held in Chicago, February 22-26, 1981).

13. U.S. Department of Commerce, *U.S. Industrial Outlook 1983*, p. 16-3.

14. American Metal Market, *Metal Statistics*, annual eds. (New York: Fairchild Publications, 1964-74).

15. Estimated from American Bureau of Metal Statistics, *Nonferrous Metal Data 1980* (New York: American Bureau of Metal Statistics, 1980).

16. American Metal Market, *Metal Statistics*, 1964-74.

17. Al Gedicks, "Raw Material Strategies of Multinational Copper Companies Based in the United States," in Ann Seidman, *Natural Resources and National Welfare: The Case of Copper* (New York: Praeger, 1975), p. 95. See also Raymond F. Mikesell, ed., *Foreign Investment in the Petroleum and Mineral Industries* (Baltimore: Johns Hopkins University Press, 1971).

18. James H. Jolly, "Copper," in U.S. Department of the Interior, Bureau of Mines, *Minerals Yearbook, 1978-79* (Washington, D.C.: U.S. Government Printing Office, 1980), p. 276.

19. Ibid.

20. See, especially, Bernhard K. Heffner, "The Potential Economic Impact of U.S. Regulations on the U.S. Copper Industry" (Washington, D.C.: U.S. Department of Commerce, Office of Business Policy Analysis, April 1979); Moshe Weiss, "The Impact of Environmental Control Expenditures on the U.S. Copper, Lead and Zinc Mining and Smelting Industry" (New York: National Economic Research Associates, January 1978); and Arthur D. Little, Inc., "Economic Impact of Environmental Regulations on the United States Copper Industry" (Report submitted to the U.S. Environmental Protection Agency, January 1978).

21. Jolly, "Copper," p. 274.

22. Heffner, "Potential Economic Impact of U.S. Regulations," pp. 1-2.

23. U.S. Department of Commerce, *U.S. Industrial Outlook 1981*, p. 210.

24. R.J. Muth, response to Conservation Foundation "Survey on Environmen-

tal Regulations and the Location of Industry" (received March 25, 1981).

25. Matthew P. Scanlon, response to Conservation Foundation "Survey on Environmental Regulations and the Location of Industry" (received March 25, 1981).

26. See D. B. Evans, "World Production and Consumption of the Major Non-Ferrous Metals 1960-1971," *World Minerals and Metals*, no. 10 (November/December 1972), p. 6 and p. 8, table 2.

27. See William A. Vogely, ed., *Economics of the Mineral Industries*, 3rd ed. (New York: American Institute of Mining, Metallurgical and Petroleum Engineers, 1976); John W. Whitney, "An Analysis of Copper Production, Processing and Trade Patterns, 1950-1972" (Ph.D. dissertation, Pennsylvania State University, Department of Mineral Economics, May 1976); and Raymond F. Mikesell, *The World Copper Industry: Structure and Economic Analysis* (Baltimore: Johns Hopkins University Press, 1981), pp. 24-27.

28. Mikesell, *The World Copper Industry*, p. 26; W.C.J. Van Rensburg and S. Bambrick, *The Economics of the World's Mineral Industries* (Johannesburg, South Africa: McGraw-Hill, 1978), p. 172; Bossan and Varon, *The Mining Industry and the Developing Countries*; and UNIDO, *Mineral Processing in Developing Countries*.

29. See Bossan and Varon, *The Mining Industry and the Developing Countries*.

30. W. G. Davenport, "Copper Smelting to the Year 2000," *Canadian Mining and Metallurgical Bulletin*, January 1980.

31. H. Dolezai et al., *Environmental Consideration for Emerging Copper-Winning Processes* (Cincinnati, Ohio: U.S. Environmental Protection Agency, Industrial Environmental Research Laboratory, 1982).

32. Mikesell, *The World Copper Industry*, p. 64.

33. Ibid., pp. 64-69.

34. See W. H. Dresher and D. W. Rodoff, "Smelter Pollution Abatement: How the Japanese Do It," *Engineering Mining Journal*, May 1981; and T. Nagano, "The History of Copper Smelting in Japan," *Journal of Metals*, June 1982. Dresher and Rodoff contend that one of the most significant factors that has differentiated the Japanese from U.S. companies in recent years is the former's emphasis on pollution abatement as the number one design consideration in planning new smelters or upgrading old ones. Nagano says that pollution-abatement efforts are 99 percent complete for Japanese smelters, but he notes that future expansion of Japanese capacity may be limited by a saturation of makets for by-product sulfur dioxide.

35. See J. G. Peacey, "Copper Production and Extractive Metallurgy in 1981," *Journal of Mining*, April 1982; and the section on copper in U.S. Department of Commerce, *U.S. Industrial Outlook 1983*, pp. 19-1 to 19-3.

36. See, especially, Davenport, "Copper Smelting to the Year 2000"; Dolezai et. al., *Environmental Considerations for Emergent Copper-Winning Processes*; and Mikesell, *The World Copper Industry*.

37. American Metal Market, *Metal Statistics 1980* (New York: Fairchild Publications, 1980), pp. 249-53.

38. U.S. Department of Commerce, *U.S. Industrial Outloook 1981*, pp. 216-17.

39. U.S. Department of Commerce, *U.S. Industrial Outlook 1983*, pp. 19-6 to 19-8.

40. American Metal Market, *Metal Statistics 1980*, p. 249, and U.S. Bureau of Mines, *Minerals Yearbook, 1978-79*, p. 989.

41. U.S. Department of Commerce, *U.S. Industrial Outlook 1981*, p. 216.

42. Ibid.

43. See J. L. Broadhead, "Zinc in the 1980's," in *Lead, Zinc, Tin* (proceedings of TMS/AIME conference, Las Vegas, Nevada, February 24-28, 1980). Broadhead reviews changes in the zinc industry from 1960 to 1978.

44. Zinc Institute, *U.S. Zinc Industry 1976* (New York: Zinc Institute, 1976).

45. U.S. Bureau of Mines, *Minerals Yearbook, 1978-79*, p. 1003.

46. Carl Hayden Cotterill, *Industrial Plant Location: Its Application to Zinc Smelting* (St. Louis: American Zinc, Lead and Smelting Co., 1950), p. 127.

47. Ibid., p. 16.

48. R. L. Stubbs, "Zinc in the Developing Areas in 1968," in Zinc Institute, *U.S. Zinc Industry 1968* (New York: Zinc Institute, 1968), p. 31.

49. See American Bureau of Metal Statistics, *Non Ferrous Metal Data 1979* (New York: American Bureau of Metal Statistics, 1980), pp. 67-83; and U.S. Bureau of Mines, *Minerals Yearbook, 1978-79*, pp. 993-97.

50. For recent perspectives, see W. A. Lemmon and D. Haliburton, "An Overview of Controls in Primary Lead and Zinc," in *Control of Particulate Emissions in the Primary Nonferrous Metals Industries* (Proceedings of a U.S. Environmental Protection Agency conference, Monterey, California, March 18-21, 1979); and J. F. Cole, "U.S. Environmental Laws and Regulations as Applied to the Lead and Zinc Industries," in *Lead, Zinc, Tin*.

51. U.S. Department of Commerce, *U.S. Industrial Outlook 1981*, p. 217.

52. See "Lead and Zinc Are Scaling the Steep Road to Recovery," *World Business Weekly*, May 4, 1981, pp. 42-43.

53. American Bureau of Metal Statistics, *Nonferrous Metals Data 1979*.

54. U.S. Department of Commerce, *U.S. Industrial Outlook 1981*, p. 212.

55. U.S. Department of Commerce, *U.S. Industrial Outlook 1983*, p. 19-5.

56. John A. Rathjen and T. John Rowland, "Lead," in U.S. Bureau of Mines, *Minerals Yearbook, 1978-79*, pp. 507-510.

57. Ibid., p. 507. See also Cole, "U.S. Environmental Laws and Regulations."

58. J. A. Wright, "Lead Industries in the 1980s," in *Lead, Zinc, Tin*.

59. U.S. Department of Commerce, *U.S. Industrial Outlook 1983*, pp. 19-3, 19-4.

60. Ibid., p. 19-5.

61. Ibid.

62. Ibid.

63. Wright, "Lead Industries in the 1980s."

64. "Minor Metals," in U.S. Bureau of Mines, *Minerals Yearbook, 1978-79*, pp. 1,033-34.

65. In fact, 97 percent of all arsenic consumed in end-product manufacture is in the form of arsenic trioxide. See Stanford Research Institute, "Arsenic Trioxide," in *Chemical Economics Handbook* (Menlo Park, Calif.: Stanford Research Institute, 1979), p. 710.2000E.

66. Ibid., pp. 710.2000E - 710.2000F. See also U.S. Bureau of Mines, *Minerals Yearbook, 1978-79*, p. 1034.

67. Stanford Research Institute, "Arsenic Trioxide," p. 710.2000F.

68. The other important producers of arsenic trioxide include a gold and silver smelter in Salsigne, France; a cobalt smelter in Penarroya, France; a lead and copper smelter in Namibia; a copper smelter in Sweden; and a copper smelter in San Luis

Potosi, Mexico. S. C. Carapella, Jr., "Arsenic and Arsenic Alloys," in *Kirk-Othmer Encyclopedia of Chemical Technology*, 3rd ed., vol. 3 (New York: Wiley-Interscience, 1978), p. 247; and U.S. Bureau of Mines, *Minerals Yearbook, 1978-79*, p. 1,036.

69. Stanford Research Institute, "Arsenic Trioxide," p. 710.2000B; and David B. Brooks, *Supply and Competition in Minor Metals* (Baltimore: Johns Hopkins University Press, 1965), p. 134.

70. See Thomas R. Navin, *Copper Mining and Management* (Tuscon, Ariz.: University of Arizona Press, 1978), pp. 169-70.

71. Stanford Research Institute, "Arsenic Trioxide," p. 710.2000C.

72. U.S. Bureau of Mines, *Minerals Yearbook, 1978-79*, p. 1036.

73. See Stanford Research Institute, "Arsenic Trioxide," p. 710.2000B; U.S. Environmental Protection Agency, *Air Pollution Assessment Report on Arsenic* (Research Triangle Park, N.C.: U.S. Environmental Protection Agency, 1976); and Roger M. Williams, "Arsenic and Old Factories," *Saturday Review*, January 20, 1979.

74. Barry I. Castleman, "The Export of Hazardous Factories to Developing Nations" (Independent report issued March 7, 1978), p. 12.

75. "Minor Metals," p. 1036.

76. Ibid.

77. Stanford Research Institute, "Asbestos" in *Chemical Economics Handbook* (1980), p. 712.1000B.

78. Ibid., p. 712.1000I. For a detailed description of the perils, see Paul Brodeur, *Expendable Americans* (New York: Viking Press, 1973).

79. See Alexander McRae, Leslie Whelchel, and Howard Rowland, eds., *Toxic Substances Control Sourcebook* (Germantown, Md.: Aspen Systems Corp., 1978), pp. 83-84.

80. See Note, "Worker's Compensation and the Asbestos Industry," *Syracuse Law Review* 33 (Summer 1982):1,073-84; Note, "The Constitutionality of a Federal Response to Asbestos Exposure," *Syracuse Law Review* 34 (Summer 1983):887-925.

81. Barney J. Feder, "Continued Asbestos Use Seen," *The New York Times*, July 6, 1981, pp. D1-D2.

82. D.R. Ray, *Economic Impact of the Ban of Certain Products Containing Free Asbestos* (Washington, D.C.: Consumer Products Safety Commission, 1977).

83. William M. Meylan et. al. "Chemical Market Input/Output Analysis of Selected Chemical Substances to Assess Sources of Environmental Contamination: Task III: Asbestos " (Report prepared for U.S. Environmental Protection Agency, Office of Toxic Substances, contract no. 68-01-3224-Task III, August 1978), pp. 107-63.

84. Ibid., pp. 193-224, 262-79.

85. Feder, "Continued Asbestos Use Seen."

86. Ibid.

87. H.B. Moreno, senior operating vice-president of Johns-Manville Corporation, quoted in "Dying for Work: Occupational Health and Asbestos, *NACLA Report on the Americas* 12, no. 2. (March-April 1978):24.

88. See ibid., pp. 24-28; and Castleman, "The Export of Hazardous Factories," p. 10.

89. See interviews with Mexican officials in "Dying for Work," pp. 23-24.

90. Quoted in H. Jeffrey Leonard, "Pollution Plagues Industry in Industrializing Nations," *Conservation Foundation Letter*, August 1982.

91. Ibid. The case is described in more detail in H. Jeffrey Leonard, "Environmental Regulations, Multinational Corporations and Industrial Development in the 1980s," *Habitat International* 6, no. 3 (1982):323-41.

92. William B. Hall and Robert E. Ela, "Cement," in U.S. Department of the Interior, Bureau of Mines, *Mineral Commodity Profile-26* (Washington, D.C.: U.S. Government Printing Office, 1978), p. 1.

93. Ibid., p. 3.

94. Ibid., p. 2.

95. James T. Dikeou, "Cement," in U.S. Bureau of Mines, *Minerals Yearbook, 1978-79*, p. 153.

96. Hall and Ela, "Cement," p. 14.

97. Ibid., p. 13.

98. Dikeou, "Cement," p. 174.

99. Ibid., p. 174; Hall and Ela, "Cement," pp. 13-14; and "Cement," in U.S. Department of the Interior, Bureau of Mines, *Mineral Commodity Summaries 1983* (Washington, D.C.: U.S. Government Printing Office, 1983), p. 28.

100. Hall and Ela, "Cement," p. 13.

101. Boston Consulting Group, "Cement," in *The Economic Impact of Pollution Control: A Summary of Recent Studies* (Washington, D.C.: U.S. Government Printing Office, 1972), p. 84.

102. Dikeou, "Cement," pp. 153, 155-56.

103. Boston Consulting Group, "Cement," p. 82.

104. Ibid., p. 79.

105. Ibid., p. 81.

106. Hall and Ela, "Cement," pp. 16-17.

107. Ibid., p. 3; and Boston Consulting Group, "Cement," pp. 83-84.

108. Dikeou, "Cement," pp. 154-157.

109. Hall and Ela, "Cement," p. 20.

110. Bossan and Varon, *The Mining Industry and the Developing Countries*, p. 185.

82

4. Chemical Industries

The depressed U.S. economic situation during the early 1980s redounded throughout the chemicals sector—dampening demand for finished chemicals for consumer goods, agricultural use, and construction; for intermediate chemicals needed in industrial production processes; and for basic chemicals needed as raw materials by virtually every industry in the United States. Yet, although overall U.S. output of basic chemicals and chemical products tapered off in the early 1980s from a high reached in 1979, the chemical sector remains a mainstay of the U.S. economy. Its growth rate in the remaining years of the decade is projected to be above the rate for manufacturing industries as a whole.

The chemical sector is divided into two parts, the inorganic (noncarbon-based) chemical industries—primarily basic commodity chemicals such as chlorine and various acids, oxides, and gases—and the organic (carbon-based) chemical industries, including, especially, primary and intermediate petrochemicals and products made from them. Fundamental differences exist in the chemistry of production of these two branches and, as well, in the harms that can be caused by the chief wastes and pollutants they generate. As a result, environmental and related regulations have affected the two groups very differently.

INORGANIC CHEMICALS

Inorganic chemicals, generally produced from minerals, are employed primarily in the production or processing of other chemical and nonchemical products. Even though most of the major inorganic chemicals produced today have been made and used for well over 100 years, the U.S. inorganic-chemical industry remains a strong, vital part of the entire industrial economy. It produces many of the large-tonnage, building-block chemicals used by virtually every industry in one form or another: sulfuric, hydrochloric, nitric, phosphoric, boric, and other acids; alkalies and chlorine; ammonia; compounds made from aluminum, potassium, and sodium; and nonpetroleum-based pigments such as titanium dioxide and zinc oxide.[1]

Most inorganics are "commodity chemicals"—standardized products manufactured in large quantities with little product differentiation. As a result, producers in the industry tend to be large companies that compete primarily on the basis of price and availability rather than new product breakthroughs or claims to superior quality. Since manufacturers must rely on reductions in production costs to maintain their competitiveness and profit margins, they tend to focus research and development efforts on engineering-process innovations that save on capital, raw material, labor, and energy costs. These costs, however, have been increasing. Producers who do not implement process innovations are likely to be more vulnerable than their competitors to those increases. Similarly, U.S. companies as a whole may be undercut if foreign producers achieve significant cost savings in these areas.

Although manufacturing processes for inorganic chemicals vary, most inorganics are produced by reacting some mineral with other chemicals in a brine or aqueous solution. The inorganic chemical is then precipitated (separated from the solution), filtered, or dried out in either aqueous or anhydrous form. In general, inorganic producers have faced two major environmental problems: controlling mists caused by the chemical reaction, and disposing of large amounts of wastewater and mud that often contain traces of spent raw materials (such as acids and metals) or catalysts (such as mercury).[2] As a result, regulations that control air and water discharges or solid-waste disposal have forced major adjustments in the operating methods of the inorganic chemical industry in recent years.[3]

In some cases, those regulations, coupled with rising raw material and energy costs, have stimulated the development of production processes that are more efficient and less polluting. For example, the "mercury-cell" process for the manufacture of chlorine, caustic soda, and caustic potash has increasingly been superseded by the "diaphram-cell" process. This new process has improved production efficiency and eliminated a need for elaborate and costly procedures for removing mercury from waste streams.[4] In addition, all major producers in the inorganic-chemical industry have now switched from graphite anodes to dimensionally stable anodes. That change has increased the capacity of electrolytic cells, thereby reducing energy consumption and enabling producers to meet control standards.[5]

But the inorganic-chemical industry—with profits already squeezed by rising production and transportation costs, as well as a generally low value-to-weight ratio—has also been hard hit by the need to make large, nonproductive expenditures to control air emissions, purify wastewater, and find new ways of disposing of solid wastes. Thus, during the late 1970s, the industry's pollution-control expenditures were estimated at over $80 million per year, well over 10 percent of total annual capital expenditures in the industry.[6]

Since comparative pricing is the major means of competition within the inorganic-chemical industry, this heavy pollution burden might have been expected to significantly harm U.S. producers, prompting many of the large firms that dominate the industry to move more of their production abroad to remain competitive with foreign producers. This response might seem especially likely since the production of bulk inorganic chemicals from domestic and imported mineral products—such as potash, phosphate rock, lime, sulfur, salt, fluorspar, and metal ores—is generally one of the first (and most easily accomplished) stages in the industrialization strategies of developing nations.[7]

Nevertheless, even though U.S. imports of inorganic chemicals have risen in recent years, there has been no across-the-board trend toward overseas relocation by U.S. inorganic-chemical producers. Several factors appear to have prevented the large additional pollution-control expenditures from having such a disruptive impact:

- An increasing share of inorganic chemicals are used "captively"—that is, for manufacturing other products within the same plant or in adjacent facilities operated by the same company.[8] Chlorine, for example, is used most heavily in the manufacture of such organic chemicals as chloromethanes, ethyl chloride, vinyl chloride, vinylidene chloride (saran wraps), trichloroethylene, allyl chloride, chloroprene, chlorohydrins, and numerous pesticides and organic dyestuffs. As a result, many large organic chemical companies carry out chlorine synthesis and chlorination as part of an integrated operation at the same site.[9]
- Many inorganics are produced in conjunction with other products (for example, chlorine and caustic soda) or as a result of raw-material inputs from other production processes (sulfuric acid is often produced from sulfur dioxide that has been captured from the stacks of smelters; hydrochloric acid can be produced from hydrogen chloride recovered as a by-product in the manufacture of chlorine-containing organic chemicals).
- Many inorganics, especially acids, are so bulky, expensive, and difficult to ship long distances that benefits accruing from potentially lower environmental expenditures at foreign production plants are offset by the costs of transporting the chemicals.[10]

All of these factors have tended to keep down international trade of many of the most important inorganic chemicals: sulfuric acid, hydrochloric acid, phosphates, and potassium and sodium compounds. Almost all of the large firms that produce the majority of inorganic chemicals in the United States have large holdings and operations abroad.[11] But, in general, chemicals produced in foreign countries by these companies are intended for sale in foreign markets, not for import into the United States. U.S. companies are not reducing their domestic production of most inorganics as they open or expand foreign facilities.

There are, however, several apparent exceptions to this overall locational stability within the inorganic-chemical industry. Most notable among them are alumina, aluminum hydroxide, uranium compounds, hydrofluoric acid, and titanium dioxide, which together accounted for more than 80 percent of the value of inorganic chemicals imported into the United States in 1980.[12] For alumina, aluminum hydroxide, and uranium compounds, rising U.S. imports are linked to raw-material considerations and other nonenvironmental factors. But it appears that, in the hydrofluoric acid and titanium dioxide industries, environmental regulations can be partially linked to trends that have caused large increases in imports in recent years.

Hydrofluoric Acid

Hydrofluoric acid is produced by reacting acid-grade fluorspar (containing not less than 97 percent calcium fluoride) with sulfuric acid in a furnace.[13] This production process results in large amounts of waste gypsum contaminated with hazardous fluorides.* In general, this waste is slurried and pumped into lagoons, where it is treated with lime to precipitate the calcium fluoride and neutralize any remaining acid. The wastewater can then be recycled or discharged, with the solids either stored on site or deposited in landfills. Even with this treatment, however, serious pollution problems often result, as small amounts of calcium fluoride remain in the solid gypsum waste.[16]

Before 1970, U.S. imports of hydrofluoric acid were negligible, amounting to less than 1,000 metric tons per year. During the 1970s, however, imports increased dramatically, reaching nearly 100,000 metric tons, or nearly one-third of domestic consumption by 1980.[17]

---

*Even without problems of toxicity, the sheer volume of waste gypsum poses many logistical problems for hydrofluoric acid producers. The magnitude of those problems can be measured by the fact that it takes about 3 pounds of sulfuric acid[14] and about 2.2 pounds of fluorspar to produce 1 pound of hydrofluoric acid.[15]

Until the mid-1970s, U.S. production of hydrofluoric acid also continued to climb, but it has dropped off in recent years. Several major plants have closed, and other companies have reduced production capacity at some of their plants. Thus, although total U.S. production capacity rose from 269,000 metric tons in 1967 to 394,000 metric tons per year in 1975, it had fallen off sharply to 257,000 tons per year by 1980 (figure 4.1).[18]

Until recently, nearly all U.S. imports of hydrofluoric acid were from Canada. Especially important were two plants operated by U.S.-based Allied Chemical's Canadian subsidiary: one in Amherstville, Ontario, with an annual capacity of 41,000 metric tons, and another in Valleyfield, Quebec, with a 6,000-metric-ton annual capacity.[19] Canada, however, has been replaced by Mexico as the major source of U.S. imports of the acid. Between 1974 and 1975, annual hydrofluoric acid imports from Mexico increased more than sevenfold, from 3.8 million to 27.5 million pounds, reflecting the first year of operation of a 68,000-metric-tons-per-year plant located at Matamoros, Mexico, and operated by a partially owned subsidiary of du Pont. In 1976, imports from Mexico leapt upward again, reaching 97.3 million pounds. Since then, they have remained above 100 million pounds per year.[20]

Hydrofluoric acid is used in the United States to manufacture fluorocarbons, organic compounds that are usually made by reacting anhydrous hydrogen fluoride with either chloroform or carbon tetrachloride. Until a few years ago, fluorocarbon production accounted for as much as 70 percent of all hydrofluoric acid consumed in the United States.[21] After a decade of rapid growth, consumption of hydrofluoric acid dropped off in the mid-1970s, when the use of fluorocarbons in aerosol sprays was sharply reduced. However, consumption of the acid has been increasing again, as fluorocarbon use in resins and elastomers, solvents and degreasing agents, stain repellents, surfactants and fire-extinguishing agents, pharmaceuticals, and foaming and blowing agents have all continued to expand.[22]

Hydrofluoric acid is also utilized to produce aluminum fluoride and synthetic cryolite for the smelting of aluminum from alumina. But, although consumption of hydrofluoric acid should continue to increase, it is unlikely to grow as fast as total production of aluminum does. Concern with economics, as well as fluoride wastes and emissions, has prompted the aluminum industry to reduce the amount of hydrofluoric acid it uses from an equivalent of up to 70 pounds per ton of aluminum produced to around 56 pounds.[23]

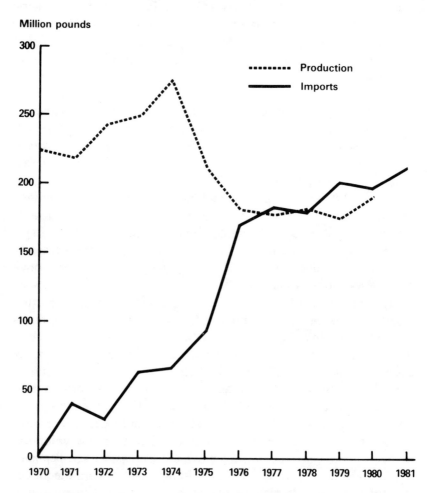

Figure 4.1
U.S. Production and Imports of
Hydrofluoric Acid, 1970–1981

Source: U.S Bureau of the Census, *U.S. Imports for Consumption and General Imports*, FT246, annual editions, TSUSA No.4162000; Standard and Poor's, "Chemicals: Basic Analysis," *Industry Surveys*, various editions.

Hydrofluoric acid has rapidly replaced sulfuric acid as the major catalyst used to react olefins (such as propylene and butylenes) with light paraffins (especially isobutane) to produce high-octane components of motor fuels.[24] It is also used in the production of uranium hexafluoride, necessary in the enrichment of uranium; in stainless steel pickling; in glassware etching and frosting; in petroleum drilling; in the production of sodium fluoride, used for water fluoridation, toothpaste, wood preservatives, and insecticides; and in the production of a wide variety of other inorganic fluorides with specialty uses ranging from the electroplating of metals to service as a catalyst in the manufacture of a nitroalkane propellant for long-range Polaris submarine missiles.[25] Nearly all of these uses are expected to increase at a healthy rate in the future, substantially pushing up overall U.S. consumption of hydrofluoric acid by the end of the 1980s.

Thus, despite concern about the use of fluorocarbons, the reduction in domestic capacity and rapid increases in imports, especially from Mexico, cannot be attributed to expected declines in domestic use of hydrofluoric acid. However, concern about pollution control, especially the disposal of the large amounts of fluoride-contaminated gypsum, has almost certainly helped influence U.S. companies to reduce domestic production and rely increasingly on imports. (A process for detoxifying and containing the contaminated gypsum wastes, consisting of dehydrating and sealing them in asphalt, has been developed for hydrofluoric acid plants, but apparently it has not been widely adopted in the United States.[26])

Several other, nonenvironmental factors also have helped make production of hydrofluoroic acid much more economically attractive overseas than in the United States. First, although the United States has substantial reserves of fluorspar and large amounts of fluorine in phosphate rock, only a small amount of these deposits are economically recoverable at current prices.[27] Instead, the major economically recoverable deposits of fluorspar are in Mexico and South Africa. In addition, transporting fluorspar before it is processed has become much more expensive in recent years—in fact, prohibitive freight costs for shipping fluorspar to the Midwest and East have been a major factor in making fluorspar mining uneconomical in the western United States.[28] Even more significant, hydrofluoric acid may be imported into the United States duty-free, but imports of unprocessed fluorspar are subject to import tariffs.[29] Major consumers of fluorspar have sought to eliminate this tariff protection for the domestic fluorspar-mining industry.[30] Their failure has only intensified the push to produce hydrofluoric acid in Mexico for shipment to the United States.[31]

Titanium Dioxide

Titanium dioxide is the largest-volume inorganic pigment and the 49th-largest-volume chemical produced in the United States.[32] It accounts for about 50 percent of all inorganic pigments consumed in this country, holds a nearly 80 percent share of the market for white pigments, and is considered a superior white pigment with no substitute of similar cost or quality, especially in regard to its brightness and its opacity (ability to block rays of light).[33]

Half the titanium dioxide consumed in the United States goes into the production of paints, with the remainder being consumed in paper coatings and fillers, plastic and rubber fillers, ceramics, and numerous incidental uses.[34] Although domestic demand for titanium dioxide fluctuated with depressed housing and construction activity during the 1970s, it has grown about 6 percent per year since the 1975 recession.[35] The trend toward precoated durable finishes in building materials may reduce the rate of increase in demand for the chemical in outdoor coatings, but anticipated increases in demand for nontoxic, latex-based interior paints, for paper products, and for plastic and other synthetic materials in containers, piping, and other durable goods should ensure healthy growth in demand for titanium dioxide pigment through the year 2000.[36]

Despite strong present and future demand for titanium dioxide, domestic producers recently have faced numerous problems that have undermined their ability to keep up with demand and compete with imports. Production of titanium dioxide pigment peaked in 1973 and 1974 at just over 1.56 billion pounds per year, but fell off during the later 1970s.[37] While consumption has topped 1.60 billion pounds in recent years, annual production has hovered around 1.40 billion pounds since 1976, although it did reach 1.57 billion pounds in 1980.[38] Thus, because consumption has grown faster than domestic production, imports, which had fluctuated from about 5 to 10 percent of domestic consumption between 1965 and 1975, have averaged nearly 15 percent of domestic consumption since then (figure 4.2).[39]

By 1978, imports had reached such an alarming level that U.S.-based SCM Corporation filed a complaint with the U.S. Department

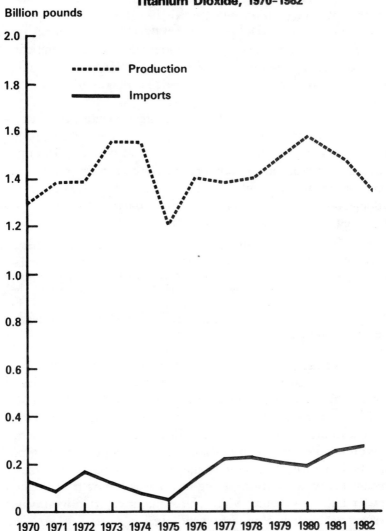

**Figure 4.2
U.S. Production and Imports of
Titanium Dioxide, 1970–1982**

Billion pounds

Source: U.S Bureau of the Census, *U.S. Imports for Consumption and General Imports*, FT246, annual editions,
TSUSA No.473700; Standard and Poor's, "Chemicals: Basic Analysis," *Industry Surveys*,
various editions.

of the Treasury alleging that producers from Belgium, West Germany, France, and the United Kingdom were selling titanium dioxide in the United States at less than fair-market value. A Treasury Department investigation determined that sales at less than fair-market value had indeed taken place, but the U.S. International Trade Commission (ITC) ruled in 1979 that those sales had not significantly injured domestic producers.[40] Nevertheless, the filing of the complaint showed the growing concern of domestic producers about the rapid increases in titanium dioxide imports.

The U.S. Department of Commerce, in its 1978 industrial outlook, noted three factors that were enabling foreign competitors to gain an increasing market hold in the United States—subsidization by foreign governments in the form of reduced taxes, tariffs, and secured loans; access to plentiful raw materials; and less-restrictive environmental constraints overseas.[41] The department's 1981 outlook elaborated on the role of environmental factors:

> Increases in the costs of producing inorganic pigments are also associated with compliance with regulations on water pollution, carcinogenicity, solid waste disposal and toxicity. . . . Plants producing TiO_2 [titanium dioxide], particularly by the sulfate process, have trouble disposing of waste. The additional costs of pollution control are shifting producers to other technologies . . .[and] have been a factor in their diminished ability to compete against imports.[42]

On the surface, there are a number of indications that the problems of U.S. titanium dioxide producers have been caused by environmental regulations. For example, two companies, PPG Industries and NL Industries, have drastically curtailed domestic production of titanium dioxide in recent years. PPG Industries, after assessing the economics of its operations and the company's marketing position, decided in 1972 to withdraw altogether from the titanium dioxide pigment business. A contributing factor was the need of the company's plants in Natrium, Virginia, for major capital investment to meet new standards for waste disposal.[43]

Since the early 1970s, NL Industries, which along with du Pont owns or controls about 35 percent of world titanium dioxide production,[44] has closed all of its U.S. production facilities, generally citing environmental factors as the major reasons. In fact, even after installing new manufacturing equipment to reduce air emissions, NL closed its last U.S. titanium dioxide facility, a 40-year-old plant in Sayreville, New Jersey, in 1982.[45]

To maintain its market share within the United States, NL has imported increasing amounts of titanium dioxide from its subsidiaries in Canada and Europe.[46] This shift of production by one company has been largely responsible for increases in overall U.S. imports of titanium dioxide.[47] With the exception of NL, the productive capacity of U.S.-based producers has remained intact in recent years, although the domestic economic situation has dampened demand for titanium dioxide by paint and pigment producers. Indeed, the industry leader in the United States, du Pont, has aggressively expanded its U.S. productive capacity during the same period that NL has shuttered its U.S. facilities.[48]

Why did NL Industries close its U.S. plants and transfer production abroad in the face of pollution regulations while du Pont expanded its U.S. production? The explanation for such different strategies pursued by the world's two largest producers and sellers of titanium dioxide, while related to the increasing stringency of U.S. environmental regulations, centers more fundamentally on technological innovation and profits.

All of the NL facilities closed in the United States used the sulfate process, which results in the formation of large amounts of waste sulfuric acid and iron sulfate. NL facilities in Norway, Canada, and West Germany continue to use this process. By contrast, several other U.S. producers, including du Pont, have pursued a strategy of shifting to the newer chloride process.[49] In fact, every titanium dioxide plant built in the United States since 1959 uses this process.[50] Thus, although the sulfate process still is used by most titanium dioxide pigment facilities in the world, a majority of U.S. production is based on the chloride process.

The chloride process uses cheaper ore as its raw material and produces far less pollution than the sulfate process. Chloride-process plants are also far more efficient than sulfate-process plants. A 1979 ITC study of the economics of the titanium dioxide industry concluded that a direct relation has existed between the profit ratios of individual companies and the percentage of their total capacity using the chloride process.[51] The ITC also pointed out: "As environmental regulations have raised the cost of disposal of pollutants and useless byproducts produced in the sulfate process, the comparative advantage of the chloride process has grown even greater."[52]

Although its strategy of shifting to overseas producers undoubtedly saved NL Industries in the short term from enormous capital expenditures to convert old sulfate-process facilities, or build new facilities, the firm will almost surely have to make such investments in the future. Not only is the chloride process more efficient, but, in addition, pollution from titanium dioxide plants has become a major political controversy throughout Europe. Public pressures, new European Economic Community regulations, and efficiency considerations will force European producers to convert their production facilities in the 1980s.[53]

ORGANIC CHEMICALS

Organic chemicals are derived from petroleum, coal, wood, or other carbon-containing matter. Although the 1970s witnessed a marked resurgence of interest in using coal, wood, and agricultural products for making basic organic-chemical feedstocks, over 90 percent of all organic-chemical production continues to originate from light (natural gas) and heavy (crude oil and its derivatives) hydrocarbons. Hence, the organic-chemical industry is heavily influenced by trends in world petroleum production, and many of the major companies that produce and sell oil or natural gas also produce organic chemicals.

This industry has grown and diversified rapidly both in the United States and worldwide since the end of World War II. Thousands of new products based on organic chemicals have been brought onto the market, replacing natural products or creating new markets of their own. Whole new industries have grown up around products made from synthetic resins and plastics, man-made fibers, and specialty chemicals; while many existing industries—for example, textiles, transportation, household cleaning, personal care, medicine, agricultural products, construction—have been revolutionized by the introduction of new synthetic organic chemicals.[54]

Less than half of the organic chemicals produced commercially in the United States in 1980 were available on a similar basis in 1940. In some specialty sectors dependent on the organic-chemical industry, the contrast is even more striking. For example, more than 90 percent of the organic products manufactured by the pharmaceutical industry today were unavailable in the early 1950s.[55]

The variety of applications and end products for organic chemicals is still expanding rapidly. For most of the 1980s, many sectors of the organic-chemical industry are expected to grow more than twice as fast as the gross national product. Dynamic demand, coupled with changing raw-material prices and supplies, means that rapid change will continue in all facets of the organic-chemical industry. Basic chemical reactions, the techniques and technologies employed in them, the raw-material inputs (and hence by-product and waste materials produced), and the many end uses will also continually change as new reactions and products are discovered and as prices, supplies, and patents evolve.[56]

In recent years, world trade in organic chemicals has grown even more quickly than has world chemical output or overall world trade. The reasons for this are complex. Many oil-rich countries and a handful of other rapidly industrializing nations, such as Brazil and South Korea, have sought to build modern petrochemical complexes of their own, both for export trade and internal use. With the incredible variety of intermediate organic chemicals necessary to operate such complexes, however, this has frequently increased both imports and exports of organic chemicals. Almost all nations—developed and developing—that do not produce the entire range of organic chemical products must import large amounts of the unproduced products for use in their modern sectors. As a result of this heavy worldwide demand for intermediate and end-use organic chemicals, the chemical industries of the advanced industrial nations have increasingly sought to expand their exports. At the same time, organic chemical trade between Western industrialized countries has also grown rapidly, as international transfers of countless intermediate chemicals within and between companies have become increasingly common.[57] Multinational corporations in the organic-chemical industry have followed the automobile and other large-scale manufacturing industries in setting up a worldwide network for producing basic, intermediate, and end-use chemicals. It is no longer unusual for one company to produce basic and intermediate organic chemicals in one country and then ship them to plants in other countries for production of end-use organic chemicals and products.

Since the United States has the largest and most diversified organic-chemical industry, the explosion of international trade in organics has, on the whole, been a boon for the U.S. economy. The organic-chemical industry and its downstream affiliates have become major export producers. Petrochemical product exports alone increased in value by 55 percent between 1975 and 1978, and they currently represent about 10 percent of all U.S. merchandise exports.[58]

Organic chemicals present major environmental problems in their production and use, in part because they are used in all segments of the economy but also because the range of pollution and workplace-health hazards associated with them is so broad. Many of these problems extend beyond the treatment or dispersion of industrial waste to reduce pollution of air, water, and land. The organic-chemical industry has had to be more concerned than many industries with consumer-related, as well as production-related, environmental problems since virtually the entire public is exposed every day to multiple organic chemical compounds in such forms as food additives, cosmetics, drugs, plastics of all kinds, and pesticides.

More and more organic chemicals have been shown to have toxic effects on humans, including such acute problems as narcosis and skin burns and such chronic problems as cancer, genetic defects, and irreversible damage to the heart, reproductive system, central nervous system, and other bodily organs. Indeed, the majority of all toxic pollutants resulting from industrial production are organic compounds. In January 1974, the Occupational Safety and Health Administration (OSHA) issued strict standards to curb workers' exposure to 14 carcinogenic chemicals, all of which were organic. Nine of the original chemicals regarded by the Environmental Protection Agency (EPA) in 1976 as toxic and subject to imminent regulation were organic compounds. Since then, the National Institute for Occupational Safety and Health (NIOSH), OSHA, and EPA and industry groups have identified over 100 organic chemicals that present potential toxic hazards and merit further investigation.[59]

In addition, synthesizing organic chemicals frequently involves reactions between volatile substances, some of which are highly explosive and some of which can be dangerous even when released into the environment in very small quantities. Moreover, many organics have demonstrated an ability to persist in the environment for long periods of time, and some chemicals, especially certain halogenated compounds, combine with other substances when released into the environment to form compounds more harmful or persistent than the chemical originally produced for industrial use.[60]

Perhaps even more important in the long term, information about the adverse effects associated with many (perhaps most) organic chemicals and products is not yet available. For example, a recent EPA attempt to summarize existing knowledge about the hazardous and toxic properties of 510 industrial organic chemicals, 142 organic dyes and pigment raw materials, 722 organic dyes and pigment intermediates, and 1,458 organic dyes and pigments noted that toxic hazard crises related to this industry are occurring with dismaying frequency. Thus a number of individual compounds (e.g., B-napthylamine, DDT, dioxin, vinyl chloride, kepone, etc.) have been first exposed as potent health or environmental hazards and then subjected to very close scrutiny, but organic chemicals as a class have only just begun to be investigated.[61]

This fact obviously adds a large degree of uncertainty to any calculations about the long-term trends of regulation, production, consumption, and importation of many organic chemicals and associated products.

As a result of all these problems, a Commerce Department report noted in 1980 that

The present forecast for developments in industry, because of these problems, is for further industry consolidation and vertical expansion. Production of difficult-to-handle chemicals that have declining markets is being terminated. Older facilities are being dismantled when regulatory standards require additional production costs that cannot be sustained by the market price. Production facilities for intermediates outside the U.S. are being used as an alternative to compliance with the regulations affecting domestic manufacture.[62]

These trends are, in fact, apparent in some of the specific instances discussed below, but they have by no means become the predominant response in the organic-chemical industry as a whole. Unquestionably, health and environmental concerns (especially about toxic and carcinogenic substances) will have major impacts on the industry. However, since rapid production innovation and technological advancement continue to be the keys to competitiveness in the industry, environmental factors are as likely to prompt new domestic development and production as they are to drive U.S. companies abroad. To a large extent, the organic chemicals and related products that have experienced declines in the face of strict environmental regulations were already on the decline when the regulations were put in place.

Primary Organic Chemicals

Primary organic chemicals are those that initially are isolated from petroleum or other raw-material feedstocks and that are themselves used as raw materials in the manufacture of a wide array of downstream organic-chemical products. Total production of primary organic chemicals in the United States has continued to grow swiftly in recent years, as demand for organic chemicals has heightened. In particular, the six most important basic organic chemicals—ethylene, propylene, benzene, toluene, methanol, and the xylenes—all experienced substantial increases in production during the 1970s; annual production now exceeds 10 billion pounds each for ethylene (by far the highest-volume organic chemical produced), propylene, benzene, and toluene. Imports of these six primary organics, over three-fourths of which come from Canada, have increased gradually, but they remain only a small fraction of overall production and are far outweighed by exports. One reason is that they are all large-volume, commodity-type chemicals that derive substantial advantages from U.S. chemical plants and complexes that tend to be bigger than those in Europe or Japan. In addition, they have benefited from U.S. prices for petrochemical feedstocks, which into the 1980s tended to be below world levels. Moreover, transport of ethylene is extremely difficult except by pipeline, inhibiting foreign trade.[63]

Thus, the high regulatory burdens facing the U.S. organic-chemical industry and numerous widely publicized battles over the siting of petrochemical complexes in the United States during the 1970s do not appear to have adversely affected the industry's international competitiveness or its ability to keep up with domestic demands for important primary organic chemicals. Of course, rapid changes in technology and product range have caused the use of some primary organics to decline precipitously in recent years. The best example is acetylene, which has been all but replaced by ethylene as one of the most basic building blocks in industrial organic chemistry. Acetylene use has declined largely because ethylene has proved safer, simpler, and cheaper to produce and to convert for downstream usage. And, since demand for acetylene has fallen off as fast as, or faster than, the chemical's production in the United States, its decline has not been accompanied by a shift to overseas production facilities.[64]

Another primary organic chemical whose use has declined in the United States is naphthalene, a suspected carcinogen primarily derived from coal tars. Naphthalene has been rapidly replaced in the United States by o-xylene as the key raw material in the production of phthalic anhydride. As a result, increased imports of naphthalene have not been needed to compensate for declining domestic production.[65]

However, environmental regulations may have helped cause the partial transfer overseas of production of at least one widely used primary organic chemical, furfural, and an accompanying major increase in imports of the chemical to the United States. Ironically, furfural is one of the few primary organics not derived from petrochemical feedstocks and not produced as part of large integrated petrochemical complexes. In addition, U.S. environmental restrictions apparently have been partially responsible for one form of another primary organic, carbon black, being increasingly produced overseas.

Furfural

Widely used as a solvent and a chemical intermediate, furfural is produced from agricultural wastes containing pentosans (complex carbohydrates). Corncobs and sugarcane bagasse are the primary raw materials used in the United States to produce this chemical, but many other waste stalks, husks, and wood pulps may also be used.[66]

Furfural's major commercial use is as a chemical intermediate in the production of furan resins, used in foundries for building metal casting molds. The resins are also used in mortars, fiberglass composites, plastic insulation foams, and refractory mixes. Another intermediate use is in the production of tetrahydrofuran, which is in turn consumed in the production of spandex fibers and polyurethane elastomers and as a solvent in polyvinyl chloride. A large amount of furfural is used as a selective extractant of undesirable aromatic compounds during the refining of lubricating oils; about 50 percent of all refineries producing finished lubricating oil now use furfural. In addition, furfural is one of several extractive solvents used to remove impurities in the production of butadiene.[67]

Three commercial processes are used around the world for producing furfural. All of them, however, hydrolyze the pentosans to pentoses by treating the raw material with strong inorganic acid and high-pressure steam. In the United States, all production is by what is known as the conventional process, which uses diluted sulfuric acid. The Rosenlew process—developed in Finland in 1968 and now used in Finland, Spain, Poland, South Africa, and the Philippines—depends upon acetic acid for hydrolysis. The other commercial process, developed in France, uses phosphoric acid. In all three processes, after hydrolysis the furfural is recovered by distillation and fractionation.[68]

Production of furfural is a bulky process. Generally, only about one-third of the pentosan content of a raw material is recovered as furfural. Thus, large amounts of wastewater containing not only inorganic acid but also partially degraded cellulose, lignin, and ash remain as by-products of furfural production.[69] Stricter land-use, waste-disposal, and water-discharge regulations in the United States in recent years have created a need for increased technological adaptations to cope with this waste.[70]

U.S. furfural production is monopolized by Quaker Oats, which is also the world's largest producer of the chemical. Quaker operates five U.S. plants with an estimated annual capacity of 216 million pounds of furfural.[71] Since Quaker is the only major U.S. producer, domestic production data has not been published by the ITC. However, it appears that U.S. production between 1974 and 1980 hovered somewhere between 90 and 100 million pounds.[72] During that period, imports of furfural skyrocketed (figure 4.3). Although imports were negligible in 1971, 1972, and 1973, they jumped to 2.6 million pounds in 1974, 12.1 million pounds in 1977, and almost 30 million pounds in 1979. Thus, imports of furfural now account for nearly one-fourth of all domestic consumption. Almost all of these imports come from the Dominican Republic, where Gulf and Western operates the world's largest furfural-producing plant.[73]

The immediate cause of these spiraling imports can be easily identified. During 1974, Quaker doubled the bulk price it charged for furfural, from 18.75 to 37 cents per pound. By December 1975, the per-pound Quaker price had reached 47 cents, and it rose again to 60 cents by 1978.[74] As a result, many U.S. consumers of furfural turned to cheaper foreign suppliers whenever possible.

Quaker cited several reasons for these drastic, rapid price increases. Direct costs of raw materials and fuel had risen much more quickly than anyone had predicted, as they had for most industries during the early 1970s. Quaker also faced increased investment costs because of construction of a new plant at Bayport, Texas; modifications required at that plant when it experienced technical difficulties; and expansions and adaptations at the company's other existing plants.[75] In addition, some of these costs were due to increased regulatory restraints and growing public concern about the environment.

But the magnitude of the price increases, which is what made imported furfural suddenly so attractive, appears to have been due primarily to Quaker's reading of the domestic supply picture. In

Figure 4.3
U.S. Imports of Furfural, 1965–1982

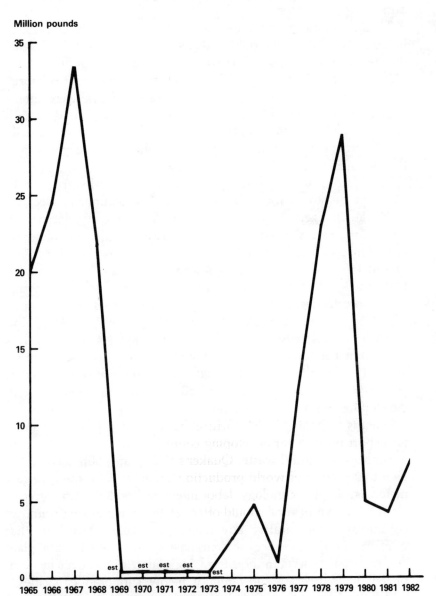

Million pounds

Furfural imports for 1969–73 were so low that they were not recorded separately.

Source: U.S. Bureau of the Census, *U.S. Imports for Consumption and General Imports*, FT 246, annual editions
TSUSA No.4275200; and Rosemary F. Bradley, "Furfural," in *Chemical Economics Handbook*
(Menlo Park, Calif.: Stanford Research Institute, 1978).

November 1973, supplies of furfural were extremely tight, with consumers placed on allocation and Quaker spurning long-term agreements and bulk discounts.[76] Even with the shift to foreign sources that followed the price hikes, Quaker's gambit probably paid off during the late 1970s.

The important question now is whether imports, which receded in the early 1980s, will erode Quaker's domestic market share again during and after the 1980s. Several factors may make it difficult for Quaker to recoup the entire U.S. market share it has lost to exports. As figure 4.3 shows, although U.S. imports of furfural were almost nonexistent in the early 1970s, they had been quite high in the 1960s. Now that Gulf and Western, because of its offshore production facility, has recaptured markets in the United States that it had held in the 1960s, it is unlikely to want to lose them.[77]

In addition, furfural is easily shipped in cans and storage tanks and may be stored for long periods of time without appreciable chemical change.[78] This factor, as well as the availability of agricultural waste materials and the relatively simple technology required in producing furfural, has led to the promotion of furfural production in several developing countries.[79] Indeed, as in the United States, world furfural-production capacity has far exceeded actual annual production and consumption in recent years. For example, world capacity was approximately 204,000 metric tons in 1978, but production was only 159,000 metric tons and consumption was 136,000 metric tons.[80] Under such circumstances, price reductions and various forms of export subsidies probably can be expected as countries try to maintain existing facilities and as new ones in other developing countries come on-line.

What is surprising is that furfural has not already become a major export product for developing countries with large amounts of available agricultural waste. Quaker's U.S. plants still account for about 40 percent of world production capacity.[81] Inexpensive raw materials, simple technology, labor intensity, and low shipping costs all indicate that furfural should offer newly industrializing countries considerable comparative advantage. It appears, however, that technical and maintenance problems have caused many furfural-plant construction projects in industrializing countries to never be completed or to operate substantially below supposed capacities.[82] Although the appropriate technology is not particularly expensive or elaborate, it is quirky. As one analysis noted, "Chemical methods leave much to be desired from the standpoint of accuracy and reproducibility."[83] Nevertheless, new and proposed plant construction in Brazil, Mexico, Kenya, China, Bolivia, India, Trinidad, and several Eastern European countries probably will increase the amounts of furfural exported from developing countries to the United States and Western Europe in coming years.[84]

Environmental regulations may be a secondary factor in this shift toward U.S. imports of furfural. But, even though U.S. regulations contributed to Quaker's major price increases for the chemical in the mid-1970s, it has never been clear whether lower pollution-control expenditures in the Dominican Republic have given Gulf and Western a significant competitive advantage. In the end, the future of U.S. predominance in furfural production will be determined, not by whether waste-disposal restrictions in developing countries are similar to those in the United States, but rather by whether the new producers can sufficiently master an unpredictable production process. If they can, they will probably maintain a price advantage over Quaker Oats's U.S. facilities.

Carbon Black

Until 1915, carbon black—gained by converting hydrocarbons into their elemental components, carbon and hydrogen—was used primarily as a pigment. Then, its qualities as a reinforcing agent, adding strength and abrasion resistance to tires and other rubber goods, were discovered. Carbon black is still used as a pigment in paints and finishes, but today more than 3 billion pounds of the substance are consumed annually as an elastomer for rubber products. On average, about 7 pounds of carbon black are used for each automobile tire made in the United States, and about 20 pounds are used for each truck tire. Large quantities are also used in molding, inner tubes, fan belts, hoses, gaskets, and numerous nonautomotive goods such as conveyor belts, floor tile, linoleum, footwear, wire coverings, coated fabrics, and mechanical goods. Carbon black serves as a reinforcing agent in paper and film goods and as a pigment and strengthener in plastic products. No satisfactory substitute for the chemical exists for many of these uses, particularly as the long-wear ingredient in tires.[85]

During the early part of this century, almost all carbon black was produced by the channel partial-combustion process—a very inefficient technology that caused severe air pollution at manufacturing sites (which were mostly located near natural gas supplies in the Southwest). With this process, only a small fraction of the carbon freed from the hydrocarbon could be recovered. As a result, the channel method caused heavy carbon-particulate emissions in thick clouds of billowing, noxious smoke.[86]

Since the 1940s, however, carbon black production methods in the United States have undergone a fundamental revolution. Now, 95 percent of U.S. carbon black is produced with the furnace partial-combustion method, which uses hydrocarbon feedstock, while the other 5 percent comes from thermal decomposition of natural gas. In 1976, the Cities Service Company closed the United States's last channel-process carbon black plant, located in Seminole, Texas. If this evolution had not occured, carbon black production in the United States probably would have been sharply curtailed in the wake of stricter air and water pollution regulations passed in the 1960s and 1970s.[87]

This changeover was motivated much more by economic factors than by concern about pollution. Both the furnace and thermal-decomposition methods yield much more recoverable carbon black per pound of hydrocarbon feedstock than does the channel method. Yet, since carbon-particulate emissions are essentially wasted production for manufacturers, and since hydrocarbon feedstocks have risen so sharply in price, ample incentives have existed for finding cleaner, more efficient means of production. The carbon black industry in the United States is today considered to be relatively free of major pollution problems. In fact, EPA water-discharge permit regulations calling for zero-level discharge by carbon black producers were not even challenged or disputed by the industry when they were issued in the late 1970s.[88]

Because the switchover to cleaner, more efficient technologies occurred before new pollution regulations curtailed carbon black production or forced a dramatic increase in production costs, there has been little push for domestic producers to shift productive facilities overseas. U.S. carbon black exports have dropped from 25 percent of domestic production to about 4 percent of production over the last 20 years, but higher pollution control costs incurred by domestic producers are not to blame. Large exports in the 1950s and 1960s were due largely to there being only a small number of carbon black plants outside of the United States. In recent years, exports have fallen off as new carbon black facilities have been built in Western Europe, Japan, and many other countries.[89]

Although U.S. imports of carbon black have always been very small compared to domestic production, imports of carbon black did grow during the 1970s, as U.S. use of the channel technology was winding down (figure 4.4). Some of this increase can be accounted for by the rapid growth in imports of channel-process carbon black from one U.S. company's production facility in Indonesia.[90] This increase in overall channel-process carbon black imports occurred because demand for channel carbon black continued even though the last few producers of channel carbon black halted U.S. production in the 1970s. For a long time, channel black was the only black coloring agent approved by the U.S. Food and Drug Administration (FDA) for use in foods (mostly licorice, jelly beans, and other candies) and cosmetics (eyebrow pencils, mascara, and nail polish). However, concern about the possible carcinogenic effects from ingestion prompted the FDA to ban the use of all carbon black in foods, drugs, and cosmetics in late 1976. As a result, channel-process carbon black imports into the United States dropped from their 1976 level.[91]

Carbon black imports do not show signs of receding to their pre-1970s levels, but it is important to point out that those imports still are equivalent to only about 1 percent of total U.S. carbon black production and that carbon black exports have been, on the average, about four times greater than imports in the early 1980s.[92] Thus, the overall rise in U.S. carbon black imports in recent years not only is largely attributable to an anomalous situation in one small end-use segment of the carbon black market but also has hardly, if at all, affected U.S. production of the chemical or the outlook for its domestic producers.

Intermediate Organic Chemicals

Organic chemicals that are produced from primary organics but undergo further chemical reactions to produce end-use chemicals and products are known as intermediate organics. The intermediate group includes both a relatively small number of chemicals produced in high volumes that provide raw materials for whole industries and a very large number of chemicals produced in small amounts for very specific uses. The high-volume intermediates, which account for over 85 percent of total intermediate production, include acetic acid, ethylene oxide, cyclohexane, ethylene glycol, ethylene dichloride, vinyl chloride, butadiene, acrylonitrile, ethylbenzene,

**Figure 4.4
U.S. Imports of Carbon Black,
1972-1982**

Million pounds

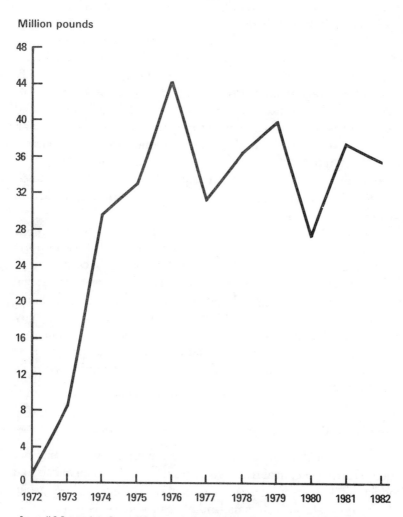

Source: U.S Bureau of the Census, *U.S. Imports for Consumption and General Imports*, FT246, annual editions,
TSUSA No.4730400.

styrene monomer, phenol, phthalic anhydride, terephthalic acid, and a handful of others.[93]

Most of these high-volume intermediate organics, like high-volume primary organics, have been experiencing rapidly expanding production. These intermediates are generally manufactured by the same companies and often in the same complexes as their precursor primary petrochemicals, so the same reasons for the continued expansion can be offered: dynamic demand; shifting price and supply pictures for raw materials; changing technologies; new discoveries about basic chemical reactions. The production increases for these intermediate organics have come about even though many of the chemicals have faced intense scrutiny from regulatory agencies and the public because of concern about their toxicity and potential carcinogenic risk.[94] (Some of the reasons why environmental regulations have not caused industrial flight for most of these chemicals are discussed in chapter 5.)

In short, U.S. exports of high-volume intermediate organic chemicals continue to be strong while U.S. imports of most of the chemicals remain equivalent to less than 1 or 2 percent of their total U.S. production.

One high-volume intermediate that has not conformed to this pattern in recent years, however, is butadiene, which is used primarily in the production of synthetic rubber products. U.S. production of butadiene has hovered between 3 and 4 billion pounds since the mid-1970s. However, U.S. butadiene imports have skyrocketed (figure 4.5) and, in 1982, were equivalent to more than 20 percent of U.S. production of the chemical. Although environmental regulations may have discouraged U.S. producers from expanding production of butadiene in recent years, Commerce Department analysts say that the main reason U.S. production levels have not risen is that less butadiene is being produced as a by-product by ethylene manufacturers. With U.S. producers of ethylene using more natural gas feedstocks (which yield less by-product butadiene), it has been easier and cheaper for U.S. butadiene consumers to import butadiene than to initiate separate and expensive production processes.[95]

Nevertheless, one intermediate for which there appears to be a link between difficulties with environmental regulations, closing of U.S. production facilities, and rapidly rising imports is thiourea. Used in photographic chemicals, flame retardants, and as a vulcanization (rubber-processing) accelerator, thiourea is a colorless liquid that has been found to cause cancer in rats and is now listed by the U.S. Department of Health and Human Services as a potential human carcinogen.[96]

Figure 4.5
U.S. Imports of Butadiene,
1972-1982

Million pounds

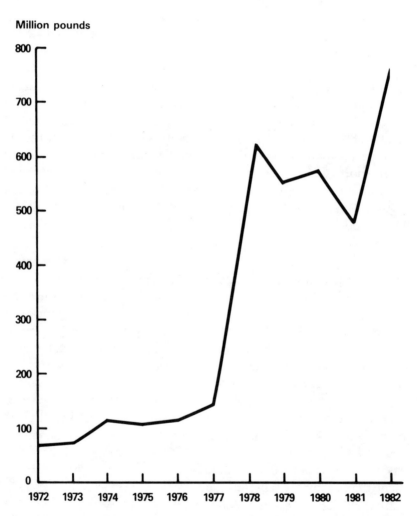

Source: U.S Bureau of the Census, *U.S. Imports for Consumption and General Imports*, FT246, annual editions, TSUSA No.4295020.

U.S. imports of thiourea and its major derivatives climbed sharply in the mid-1970s, reaching nearly 20 million pounds in 1977 (figure 4.6). It is estimated that domestic production at this time was about 5 million pounds per year.[97] By 1979-80, no producers of thiourea remained in the United States, although EPA found about 70 companies importing the chemical,[98] primarily from Japan, Belgium, the Netherlands, and West Germany.[99] Nevertheless, imports have dropped off substantially since 1977 as U.S. demand for thiourea has declined because of OSHA and EPA restrictions and the increased use of substitute chemicals.

In addition to the large-volume intermediate organic chemicals, over 1,000 other intermediates are produced in low volumes by the U.S. chemical industry.[100] Overall, U.S. imports of these chemicals remain low, although some of these intermediates recently have experienced steady and sometimes rapid increases in imports. Annual imports of others have fluctuated. Measuring all the reasons for the international shifts in production is difficult, however, since many of these chemicals, unlike high-volume intermediates, are produced by only a few U.S. producers. Frequently, only one company manufactures the chemical.[101]

An important subgroup of these low-volume intermediate chemicals are those belonging to the benzenoid family. The term *benzenoid chemical* is applied to cyclic (symmetrical in structure) organic chemicals with a benzene nucleus and to a large number of organic compounds derived from the parent benzenoid chemical. Many of the organic chemicals that have been associated with high toxicity, potential carcinogenic effects, or other health and environmental hazards belong to the benzenoid group. Thus, examination of imports of benzenoid intermediates may yield significant clues about overall trends among problem chemicals in the organic intermediate chemicals group.

Total imports of benzenoid intermediates have fluctuated in recent years, between 200 and 400 million pounds (figure 4.7). These imports account for only a small portion of total U.S. consumption of these chemicals. (It is difficult to compile production figures to match the ITC's compilation of imported benzenoid intermediates, but imports have probably been equivalent to between 1 and 3 percent of U.S. production).[102]

However, U.S. imports of several dozen of the benzenoid intermediates have risen even more substantially during the past decade.

**Figure 4.6
U.S. Imports of Thiourea,
Thiourea Dioxide, and Related
Derivatives, 1972–1979**

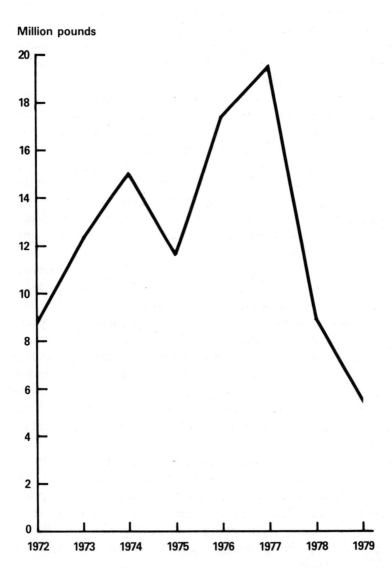

Million pounds

Source: U.S Bureau of the Census, *U.S. Imports for Consumption and General Imports*, FT246, annual editions, TSUSA No.4253660.

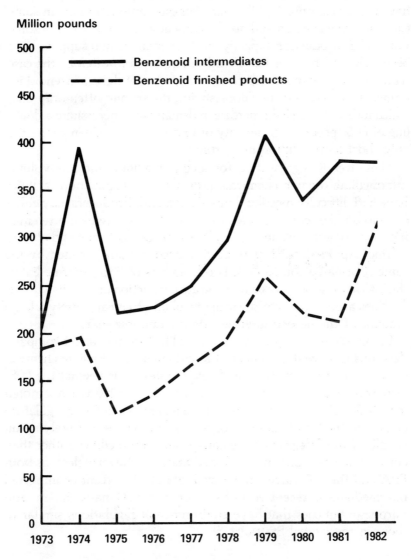

Figure 4.7
U.S. Imports of Benzenoid Intermediates and
Finished Benezenoid Products, 1973-1982

Million pounds

Benzenoid intermediates

Benzenoid finished products

Source: U.S. International Trade Commission, *Imports of Benzenoid Chemicals and Products*,
USITC Publication 1401, annual editions, 1973-82.

Even though it is difficult to ferret out the exact reasons for the rises in imports of many of these chemicals, three observations are possible. First, the statistics that are available indicate that U.S. production for most of these benzenoid chemicals has remained relatively stable or risen slowly in recent years.[103] Second, where demand figures or estimates for the United States are available, demand appears to have increased more rapidly than domestic production or, in some cases, to have gone up and down erratically, meaning that, in some years, U.S. production capacity has been strained and supplies have been tight.[104] Third, as has already been noted to often be the case with low-volume intermediate organics, most of these benzenoid intermediates have very few domestic producers and often only one, which means that a slight increase in demand may necessitate a doubling of U.S. production capacity or imports in any given year—the only short-term solution in a crunch.

These trends suggest that, for several medium- and low-volume intermediate organic chemicals, existing U.S. production facilities have had difficulty meeting domestic demand. Producers may either have to build or convert new production facilities (which often may increase domestic production by 50 to 100 percent) or to go abroad to find supplies (which may be produced in plants owned by the same U.S.-based companies). For producers of these intermediates, the logical decision may be to integrate production among its various facilities around the world, since one plant often can supply a large amount of the needed intermediate for multiple markets.

In some of these cases, environmental factors may affect company decisions to have the supplier of a particular intermediate chemical be overseas rather than in the United States. This is what the U.S. Department of Commerce was referring to in 1980 when it noted in its *U.S. Industrial Outlook* that, because of the tightening regulatory climate in the United States, some U.S. companies were relying on supplies from foreign intermediate-production facilities rather than constructing new ones in the United States.[105] Nevertheless, as both EPA and the ITC have emphasized, about 90 percent of imported intermediates in recent years have come from Canada, Japan, and Europe—countries that have environmental regulations similar to those in the United States.[106]

Finished Organic Chemical Products

Finished organic chemical products are those that are manufactured chiefly from primary and intermediate organics and that are sold directly for consumption (for example, detergents, pharmaceuticals, pesticides, photographic and other special-use chemicals) or are used in final form by other industries (rubber, plastics, resins, dyes and pigments, flavors and perfumes, synthetic fibers). In many instances, there are relatively few pollution and workplace-health problems associated with the manufacturing of finished products, either because potential problems have been "left behind" at the primary or intermediate level or because a volatile or dangerous chemical has already been processed or polymerized into more stable state. (Polyvinyl chloride pipe is a good example.) Therefore, facilities for manufacturing finished organic products probably have been disrupted or moved abroad even less than have plants for producing primary and intermediate organic chemicals.

Nevertheless, in some instances, notably the dye industries and the pesticides industry, the pollution and workplace-health problems may be little reduced, or even more acute, at the finished product stage of manufacturing than during the production of the organic building blocks that go into the finished products. In such cases, the chances are greatly increased that an industry will move its entire production process overseas from the derivation of primary organics to the synthesis of intermediates and finished chemical products.

Benzidine-Based Dyes

Benzidine and two of its related compounds, o-tolidine and o-dianisidine, constitute a family within a class of chemicals called synthetic aromatic amines. These three compounds are used as raw materials in the manufacture of azo dyes for textiles, leathers, and paper products. At least 400 dyes, known collectively as benzidine-congener dyes, have been synthesized from these compounds, although many of them are no longer commercially produced.[107]

The use and manufacture of benzidine has been associated with a high risk of bladder cancer among exposed workers for over 60 years.[108] Both o-tolidine and o-dianisidine have been shown to be carcinogenic in laboratory animals, although they have not been directly implicated as human carcinogens. These two materials generally are produced in the same chemical plants as benzidine and with similar processes, so isolated studies of worker exposure to them have been difficult to conduct.[109] However, since regulation and concern has focused until recently primarily on benzidine and benzidine-related compounds, data presented below also concentrate on raw benzidine and benzidine-based dye imports and production.

Until a few years ago, most concern about benzidine dyes focused on the use of the raw materials, especially benzidine, before and as they were mixed with the dyes' other ingredients. The major danger was thought to be from the uncombined benzidine that workers were exposed to and that was discharged with waste effluents from production sites.[110] It was thought that, once the raw materials were combined with other substances in finished dyes, they posed fewer serious health hazards. Now, however, concern has been directed toward the dangers associated with the levels of free benzidine that can remain uncombined in finished dyes.[111] Even more significant, it has been discovered that many benzidine-based and benzidine-cogener dyes are metabolized by the human body upon contact, resulting in their conversion back to the carcinogenic raw materials. In fact, a 1979 U.S. government bulletin warned that at least three benzidine-based dyes should be treated as if they were raw benzidine in terms of their potential carcinogenicity.[112] In 1980, OSHA and NIOSH jointly issued a health hazard alert covering benzidine, o-tolidine, and o-dianisidine dyes.[113]

These concerns have led to a cessation of all raw benzidine production in the United States and several other advanced industrial countries, including Sweden, Great Britain, Italy, Japan, and Switzerland. The last two commercial manufacturers of raw benzidine in the United States ceased production in 1977. (Before 1975, several million pounds of benzidine had been produced in the United States annually.) A 1979 consultant's report on the manufacture, use, and importation of benzidine-based dyes concluded unequivocally that "OSHA regulation is the reason for the cessation of benzidine production for commercial purpose."[114]

Despite the potential problems with residual free benzidine, some dye manufacturers in the United States have continued to produce benzidine *in situ* in fabricating their dyes, and a variety of closely related substances—especially 3,3'-Dichloro-benzidine and 3,3'-Dimethylbenzidine—have remained in commercial use for production of benzidine-based dyes.[115] Still, the number of U.S. firms manufacturing these benzidine and benzidine-related dyes in recent years has diminished; at least 15 domestic producers stopped producing benzidine-based dyes between 1973 and 1979.[116]

More than half of all dyes that have experienced reduced or discontinued production and use because of safety problems and regulatory restraints on benzidine have been "direct dyes," a class of dyes characterized by their negatively charged electrons and used for cellulosic fibers, paper, and leather.[117] Examination of production and import figures for direct dyes, and comparison of those figures with trends in the dye industry as a whole, provide significant evidence that U.S. dye manufacturers have turned increasingly to foreign suppliers in recent years as U.S. production of benzidine-based dyes has wound down. U.S. imports of direct dyes have climbed steeply since 1975 (figure 4.8). This rapid expansion has occurred in spite of the fact that total U.S. imports of all dyes totaled about 30.5 million pounds in both 1973 and 1982 (although there was some fluctuation in overall dye imports during that decade). Thus, the share of direct dyes in U.S. dye imports has risen substantially, from 3.3 percent in 1973 to 10.9 percent in 1982.[118] Since U.S. production of direct dyes stabilized during the late 1970s, averaging about 31.25 million pounds, imports now represent a much higher share of U.S. consumption of direct dyes: in 1977, imported direct dyes equaled only 3.4 percent of U.S. production, but, by 1982, they had grown to be equivalent to 10.2 percent of U.S. production.[119]

This dramatic rise in direct-dye imports is a clear indicator that environmental and workplace-health regulations, coupled with labor-union concerns for worker health, are fundamentally disrupting U.S. production of raw benzidine, benzidine-related compounds, and their derivative dyes. In most cases, it appears that former U.S. producers of these dyes have not themselves transferred production overseas. Instead, they have relied on foreign producers, especially from Western Europe, to supply the dyes.[120] In addition, new producers in such industrializing countries as Egypt, India, Poland, and Romania have grabbed a growing share of the U.S. benzidine dye market. Most notable among those countries has been India, which accounted for 0.7 percent of the total value of overall U.S. dye imports in 1973. That share has grown steadily since then, reaching 4 percent in 1982.[121]

With an increasing number of finished products containing benzidine-related dyes being banned from sale in the United States, and with virtually all U.S. dye producers searching for safer dye substitutes, the use of benzidine-related dyes is expected to decline in the future.[122] Thus, it seems expedient for U.S. producers to import supplies of those dyes to meet domestic market demand for a declining product. *

---

*Obviously, this indicates that growing import penetration of U.S. markets for direct dyes may prove to be less of a boon to foreign producers in the long run

Figure 4.8
U.S. Imports of Direct Dyes, 1973-1982

Million pounds

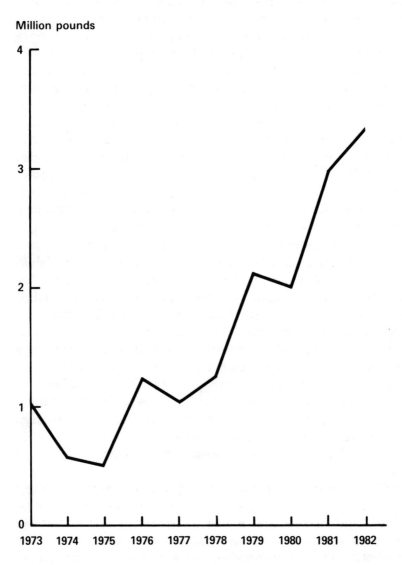

Source: See figure 4.6.

Pesticides

The pesticide industry is a relatively mature one, with overall demand expected to grow relatively slowly in coming years.[125] Yet the U.S. pesticide industry has been in a constant state of flux, introducing new products at a rapid rate and generating profits and growth opportunities for many manufacturers.

One reason for the continued strength of the pesticide industry is that growth in the herbicide group has been particularly dynamic in recent years, offsetting slow growth for insecticides and fungicides. But there are several other reasons as well. First, many pesticides, especially insecticides, are subject to a natural process of biological obsolescence—over time, pests become able to tolerate them. As a result, producers must constantly be developing new products.[126] Second, concerns about the toxicological effects and persistence of pesticides in the ecosystem and in living tissue have led to regulations banning some pesticides and restricting application of others. This, in turn, has stimulated greater research to develop new, less persistent pesticides.[127] Third, demand for pesticides overseas, both in developed and developing countries, has continued to expand, enabling exports to account for a major share of total U.S. pesticide production—up to 25 percent in recent years.[128] This demand for U.S. exports has been especially beneficial to U.S. producers, since other countries frequently have absorbed products that either have almost become biologically obsolescent in the United States or have had their usage restricted by domestic regulations.**

---

than appears to be the case now. This long-term outlook for importers is reinforced by the fact that U.S. consumer-protection laws and import standards have proven to pose difficulties for some foreign producers. Indeed, some countries (notably Romania) have already lost export markets to the United States because of quality-control problems. Romanian dyes have contained as much as 1,000 parts per million of free benzidine,[123] compared to an average of less than 20 parts per million in dyes produced in the United States.[124]

**The potential dangers to recipient countries caused by their importing of pesticides that are heavily regulated or no longer used in the United States have received much publicity in recent years.[129] One study found that almost 25 percent of the approximately 600 million pounds of pesticides exported from the United States were not registered for use in the United States. About 31 million pounds of these exports were of pesticides whose registrations had been canceled by the EPA because of the health and environmental hazards they posed.[130]

The constant product evolution caused by these trends has, in general, led to higher priced, less persistent, less toxic pesticides being offered in the United States, while older, cheaper, more persistent, and more toxic products are exported. Thus, the domestic market share held by organophosphate-based pesticides has expanded in recent years, while organochlorines have declined significantly in use in the United States.[131] However, chlorinated pesticides (for example, DDT [dichloro-diphenyl-trichloro-ethane], aldrin/dieldrin, and 2,4-D) continue to be important export products for U.S. manufacturers, with exports now accounting for two-thirds of U.S. organochlorine-pesticide production.[132]

The overall pesticide industry continues to generate a very positive trade balance—with the total value of exports exceeding the value of imports by about an 8 to 1 margin in recent years[133]—and few U.S. producers have opened facilities overseas to manufacture pesticides for marketing in the United States. Still, some segments of the pesticide industry have experienced considerable increases in imports in the last decade. These trends are particularly apparent for pesticides derived from benzenoid chemicals. Recently, these pesticides have accounted for about 58 percent of the total volume, and a slightly higher percentage of the total value, of annual pesticide production in the United States.[134] However, a far larger share of U.S. pesticide imports—almost 90 percent—are benzenoid pesticides.[135]

Imports of benzenoid pesticides have grown very quickly during the past decade, from just over 24 million pounds in 1973 to nearly 102 million pounds in 1982 (figure 4.9). This increase becomes even more striking when it is measured as a percentage of U.S. production of benzenoid pesticides. In 1977, for example, benzenoid-pesticide imports were equivalent to only 5 percent of the 830 million pounds of benzenoid pesticides produced in the United States. By 1982, with U.S. production having dropped to 645 million pounds, imports equaled 15.8 percent of U.S. benzenoid-pesticide production by volume.[136]

Like benzenoid organic intermediates, many benzenoid pesticides have been particularly hard-hit by U.S. environmental and workplace-health regulations because of their toxicity. Although it is very difficult to find the specific reason for rising imports for each of the hundreds of benzenoid pesticides that are imported into the United States, there may be reason to conclude that U.S. regulations

Figure 4.9
U.S. Imports of Benzenoid Pesticides,
1973-1982

Million pounds

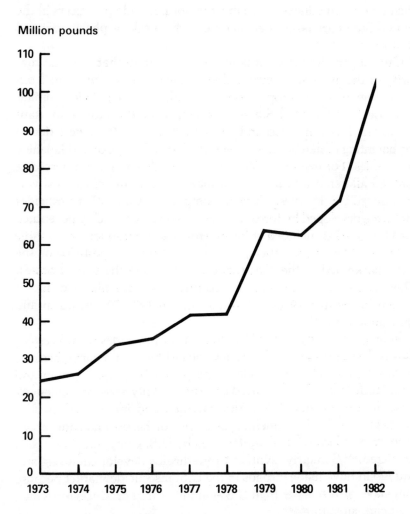

Source: U.S International Trade Commission, *Imports of Benzenoid Chemicals and Products*, U.S. ITC
Publications 1401, annual editions, 1973–82.

have been a factor in the overall increase of benzenoid-pesticide imports. Such a conclusion can seem even more likely when one considers the already-cited evidence that U.S. companies have relied more heavily on overseas facilities for supplies of certain benzenoid chemical intermediates, since most major pesticide producers in the United States are large chemical, petrochemical, or pharmaceutical companies.[137]

Once again, however, it is important to note that the vast majority of the increased benzenoid-pesticide imports have come from facilities in Western Europe and Japan, which have regulations similar to those in the United States. For several of the most important pesticides, rapid increases in U.S. imports in the 1970s were due to the patenting of new, innovative pesticides by European and Japanese companies. For example, Bentazon, the trade name for a herbicide that led all benzenoid-pesticide imports during the mid-1970s, was introduced by the West German company BASF. Other pesticides that were developed by foreign companies and that quickly penetrated the U.S. market included chlordimeform and paraquat. In all three instances, like several others, the success of the new pesticide on the U.S. market led to the construction of plants in the United States. Thus, declines in U.S. imports occurred as these plants came on stream in the mid-1970s (paraquat) and in 1979-80 (bentazon and chlordimeform).[138]

In fact, one irony is that U.S. imports of pesticides from Western Europe have grown rapidly during the last few years partly because of heavy research and development efforts by West German and Swiss companies that produced environmentally safer pesticides. As a result, several new herbicides patented and introduced in U.S. markets have been commercial successes for European producers as more harmful products manufactured by U.S. companies have been restricted.[139] Similarly, synthetic pyrethroids developed in England and Japan have made inroads in the U.S. insecticide market because they have proven safer than U.S.-manufactured products for which they can substitute.[140]

Another reason that U.S. imports of several old high-volume pesticides have risen is that the 17-year period of patent protection for U.S. manufacturers has expired for older pesticides. Foreign companies, freed from the need to pay licensing fees, have stepped up sales of these products in the U.S. market. For example, patent protection expired during the 1970s for two urea herbicides—diuron and linuron—that had held key market shares for du Pont.[141] Since then, U.S. imports of these two herbicides have been high. Du Pont appears to have sought to maintain its market shares by producing more of the herbicides at plants in Mexico, Colombia, and Europe, but companies in several Western and Eastern European countries and in Israel have also stepped up production of diuron and linuron since the patents expired.[142] It is, of course, possible that decreased expenditures on environmental controls have been a part of the cost savings achieved by du Pont in producing more at its overseas plants, but the loss of proprietary rights was clearly the primary cause of the locational changes that took place in the 1970s.

Another production-location change linked to the expiration of a patent for a leading herbicide appears to be occurring during the 1980s. Treflan, a major source of profits for Eli Lilly since its introduction in the early 1960s, became an off-patent herbicide in the early 1980s.[143] Several foreign producers apparently were prepared to capture an increased share of the U.S. market with generic versions of the compound, trifluralin, because U.S. imports, after several years of being too low to be registered separately, jumped to over 7 million pounds in 1982. Presumably, cheaper generic imports eventually will capture a major share of U.S. sales of trifluralin.

But some instances of expanded imports can be linked to environmental factors. U.S. imports of 2,4,5-T (2,4,5-trichlorophenoxyacetic acid) and 2,4,5-TCP (2,4,5-trichlorophenol) climbed during the mid- and late 1970s and continued to rise at high rates in the early 1980s, even though domestic demand for these herbicides fell as many of their uses were suspended by EPA.[144] Domestic production of these pesticides, however, dropped even faster than did demand as the manufacturing of both 2,4,5-T and 2,4,5-TCP came under increased scrutiny. (Producing these pesticides yields, as a byproduct, small amounts of dioxin, a powerful carcinogen.[145]) With demand for 2,4,5-T and 2,4,5-TCP also certain to continue its decline, U.S. manufacturers of both pesticides (primarily Dow Chemical) appear to be willing to draw on supplies from their overseas production facilities until a market no longer exists in the United States.

With some pesticides, U.S. imports increased dramatically immediately after U.S. production was halted during the 1970s because of environmental problems. A good example is lindane (hexachlorocyclohexane), a known carcinogen. This insecticide was produced in the United States through 1976, but both strict OSHA workplace standards on exposure and EPA limitations on waste concentrations helped stop all U.S. production by 1977.[146] Since EPA-proposed limitations on lindane use did not substantially reduce U.S. consumption for several more years, lindane imports jumped tenfold from 1976 to 1977 and doubled again in 1978. Since then, U.S. imports of lindane have tapered off as registration for many uses has been suspended.[147]

Another pesticide whose imports fluctuated up, then down, as a result of U.S. regulation in the late 1970s was DBCP (1,2-Dibromo-3-chloropropane), an effective and inexpensive soil fumigant (nematicide) for agricultural crops. DBCP was widely used until serious human health problems (such as sterility) were associated with its manufacture, formulation, and application.[148] Not only was DBCP used extensively in the United States, but annual exports before 1977 were estimated at between 30 and 40 million pounds, mostly to Central and South America for use with coffee, banana, and pineapple crops.[149]

Like lindane (although unlike many other canceled or restricted pesticides), DBCP had its production disrupted by U.S. regulations before its domestic use was completely canceled. When it was revealed in 1977 that a large number of chemical workers in several DBCP-formulating plants had a zero sperm count, OSHA quickly issued workplace-health standards that were so stringent that all U.S. production was discontinued.[150] However, EPA continued to permit certain uses of DBCP for several years. Thus, two producers in Mexicali, Mexico, were sending several million pounds of DBCP per year to a U.S. company, Amvac, for sale in the United States.[151] Additional U.S. imports were also received from an Israeli producer.[152] This situation proved to be temporary, however, with the Israeli company ceasing production of DBCP later in 1977 because of the workplace hazards. In 1979, EPA banned all domestic uses of DBCP except for pineapple growing in Hawaii, drastically cutting demand in the United States.[153] In addition, the Mexicali plants were shut down on several occasions in response to public pressures on Mexican officials and reports of high rates of sterility among plant workers.[154] Ironically, DBCP was replaced in most of its uses by EDB (ethylene dibromide), which in 1983 and 1984 was the subject of intense public concern as a potential carcinogen believed to be contaminating many food products in the United States.

Another example of a dangerous pesticide whose production has ceased in the United States but which has been imported in recent years is the insecticide dicofol. Until 1984, about two million pounds of dicofol were being imported each year for use on cotton, citrus fruits, household plants, and vegetables. EPA finally acted to curb these imports when it discovered that the insecticide contains high concentrations of DDT, which has been banned in the United States since 1972.[155]

The problems exemplified by dicofol, lindane, and DBCP are likely to recur for a number of other pesticides originally developed and registered in the 1950s and 1960s. As more of these are subjected to stringent tests not required when they were registered, more are likely to come under tighter regulatory control. In such cases, U.S. producers may find it expedient to shift production abroad in anticipation of a decline in U.S. demand.

CONCLUSIONS

Only a few U.S. industries within either branch of the chemical-manufacturing sector have increased production overseas as a direct or indirect result of environmental regulations. Virtually no disruptions of domestic production of major inorganic chemicals have been caused by regulations, although a few minor examples of movement abroad can be linked in part with U.S. environmental regulations. Among the organic chemical industries, the environmental problems are extremely complex, as are the long-term locational trends. Generally speaking, organic chemicals will constitute a major growth sector in coming years, but a few primary and intermediate chemicals may undergo declines in use or may increasingly be produced abroad. The organics branch is constantly changing, and environmental regulations may be one factor in speeding up ongoing cycles of innovation and obsolescence. Moreover, environmental hazards have caused production of some finished organic products—a few pesticides, various dyes—to be banned or virtually abandoned in the United States. Manufacture of these products abroad, or temporary increases in U.S. imports of them, may occur during the 1980s, although in the long term they will be replaced altogether.

REFERENCES

1. For background, see Mary K. Meegan, ed., *Kline Guide to the Chemical Industry*, 3rd ed. (Fairfield, N.J.: Charles Kline and Co., 1977).

2. See Marshall Sittig, *Inorganic Chemical Industry: Processes, Toxic Effluents*

and Pollution Control (Park Ridge, N.J.: Noyes Data Corp., 1978), for a description of environmental-control considerations in the production of 130 inorganic chemicals.

3. "Chemicals: A Survey," *The Economist*, April 7, 1977, p. 8.

4. U.S. Department of Commerce, *U.S. Industrial Outlook 1980* (Washington, D.C.: U.S. Government Printing Office, 1980), p. 131.

5. Standard and Poor's, "Chemicals: Basic Analysis," *Industry Surveys*, November 6, 1980, p. C-16.

6. Sittig, *Inorganic Chemical Industry*, p. 1.

7. U.S. Department of Commerce, *U.S. Industrial Outlook 1980*, p. 121.

8. U.S. Department of Commerce, *U.S. Industrial Outlook 1981* (Washington, D.C.: U.S. Government Printing Office, 1981), pp. 136-37.

9. See Peter Wiseman, *An Introduction to Industrial Organic Chemistry* (New York: Halsted Press, 1976), pp. 111-42.

10. U.S. Environmental Protection Agency, *Economic Impact Analysis of Proposed Section 5 Notice Requirements: Support Document*, Appendix: vol. 2, EPA-560/12-80-005-B, September 1980, pp. E-64-66.

11. Ibid. p. E-57.

12. U.S. Department of Commerce, *U.S. Industrial Outlook 1981*, pp. 140-41.

13. C. K. Quan, *Fluorine*, Mineral Commodity Profiles no. 20 (Washington, D.C.: U.S. Bureau of Mines, 1978), pp. 7-8. For a complete description of the production process for hydrofluoric acid, see A. J. Rudge, *The Manufacture and Use of Fluorine and Its Compounds* (London: Oxford University Press, 1962), pp. 10-18.

14. Stanford Research Institute, "Fluorine Products," in *Chemical Economics Handbook* (Menlo Park, Calif.: Stanford Research Institute, 1979), p. 739.1000E.

15. Quan, *Fluorine*, p. 7.

16. Sittig, *Inorganic Chemical Industry*, p. 158.

17. U.S. Department of Commerce, Bureau of the Census, *U.S. Imports for Consumption and General Imports*, Report FT246 (Washington, D.C.: U.S. Government Printing Office, various years), Product no. 4162000.

18. Stanford Research Institute, *1980 Directory of Chemical Producers: USA* (Menlo Park, Calif.: Stanford Research Institute, 1980).

19. Stanford Research Institute, "Fluorine Products," p. 739.1000J.

20. U.S. Bureau of the Census, *U.S. Imports for Consumption and General Imports*.

21. Quan, *Fluorine*, p. 8.

22. Ibid. See also Stanford Research Institute, "Fluorine Products," p. 739.100W, which predicts renewed growth in fluorocarbon consumption in the 1980s unless new restrictions are passed.

23. See G. D. Bruno, "Fluorine Consumption Trends in the Aluminum Industry," *Mining Engineering* 30, no. 11 (November 1978): 1,562-64, and Dennis S. Kostick and Ronald J. DeFilippo, "Fluorspar," in U.S. Department of the Interior, Bureau of Mines, *Minerals Yearbook, 1978-79* (Washington, D.C.: U.S. Government Printing Office, 1980), pp. 345-46.

24. Stanford Research Institute, "Fluorine Products," p. 139.1000Y.

25. Quan, *Fluorine*, pp. 8-9.

26. Sittig, *Inorganic Chemical Industry*, p. 158.; and Stanford Research Institute, "Fluorine Products," p. 739.1000E.

27. Quan, *Fluorine*, pp. 10-11. Quan also says that, in addition to the difficulties of recovering many U.S. fluorspar- and fluorine-containing phosphate rock deposits, U.S. labor costs and mining restrictions have helped to make fluorspar mining less economical in the United States (ibid., pp. 20-21).

28. Ibid., p. 20.

29. The duty for acid-grade fluorspar is $2.07 per metric ton, $2.10 per long ton, and $1.875 per short ton. Stanford Research Institute, "Fluorine Products," p. 739.1001G.

30. Quan, *Fluorine*, p. 20.

31. The Stanford Research Institute, "Fluorine Products," analysis says, "There is no duty on imports of hydrofluoric acid; this fact (as well as proximity to raw materials, pollution regulations, and other factors) undoubtedly had some influence on the decision to produce hydrofluoric acid in Mexico for export" (p. 739.1001H).

32. Standard and Poor's, "Chemicals: Basic Analysis," p. C-15.

33. U.S. Department of Commerce, *U.S. Industrial Outlook 1981*, p. 158.

34. Standard and Poor's, "Chemicals: Basic Analysis," p. C-15.

35. Langtry E. Lynd and Ruth A. Hough, "Titanium," in U.S. Bureau of Mines, *Minerals Yearbook, 1978-79*, p. 935.

36. Robert E. Davenport and F. Alan Ferguson, "Titanium Dioxide Pigments," in *Chemical Economics Handbook* (1978), pp. 788.5000C, D, E; and Langtry E. Lynd, *Titanium*, Mineral Commodity Profiles no. 18 (Washington, D.C.: U.S. Bureau of Mines, 1978), pp. 16-17.

37. Davenport and Ferguson, "Titanium Dioxide Pigments," p. 788.5003A.

38. Lynd and Hough, "Titanium," p. 935.

39. Ibid.

40. U.S. International Trade Commission, *Titanium Dioxide from Belgium, France, the United Kingdom and the Federal Republic of Germany* (Washington, D.C.: U.S. International Trade Commission, November 1979).

41. As cited in U.S. Environmental Protection Agency, *Economic Impact Analysis*, p. E-48.

42. U.S. Department of Commerce, *U.S. Industrial Outlook 1981*, p. 159.

43. "PPG Pulls Out of Titanium," *World Minerals and Metals*, no. 5 (January/February 1972):29.

44. Lynd, "Titanium," p. 2.

45. U.S. Department of Commerce, *U.S. Industrial Outlook 1983* (Washington, D.C.: U.S. Government Printing Office, 1983), p. 12-4.

46. U.S. International Trade Commission, *Titanium Dioxide from Belgium, France, the United Kingdom and the Federal Republic of Germany*, pp. 5-7.

47. Davenport and Ferguson, "Titanium Dioxide Pigments," p. 788.5003A.

48. U.S. International Trade Commission, *Titanium Dioxide from Belgium, France, the United Kingdom and the Federal Republic of Germany*, p. A-9.

49. Davenport and Ferguson, "Titanium Dioxide Pigments," pp. 788.5004H.-788.5004T.

50. Ibid., p. 788.5001E.

51. U.S. International Trade Commission, *Titanium Dioxide from Belgium, France, the United Kingdom and the Federal Republic of Germany*, p. 10.

52. Ibid., p. 5.

53. Davenport and Ferguson, "Titanium Dioxide Pigments," p. 788.5004I.

54. See Wiseman, *An Introduction to Industrial Organic Chemistry*, pp. 111-42.

55. "Chemicals: A Survey," p. 8.

56. Standard and Poor's, "Chemicals: Basic Analysis."

57. "Chemicals: A Survey," pp. 8ff.

58. Standard and Poor's, "Chemicals: Basis Analysis."

59. See Alexander McRae, Leslie Whelchel, and Howard Rowland, eds., *Toxic Substances Control Sourcebook* (Germantown, Md.: Aspen Systems Corporation, 1978), and U.S. Environmental Protection Agency, Industrial Environmental Research Laboratory, *Potentially Toxic and Hazardous Substances in the Industrial Organic Chemicals and Organic Dyes and Pigment Industries* (Cincinnati, Ohio: Industrial Environmental Research Laboratory, 1980).

60. McRae, Whelchel, and Rowland, *Toxic Substances Control Sourcebook*, and U.S. Environmental Protection Agency, *Potentially Toxic and Hazardous Substances*.

61. U.S. Environmental Protection Agency, *Potentially Toxic and Hazardous Substances*, p. 8.

62. U.S. Department of Commerce, *U.S. Industrial Outlook 1980*, p. 125.

63. See Standard and Poor's, "Chemicals: Basic Analysis."

64. Indeed, U.S. exports of acetylene have increased rapidly in the last decade. See, U.S. Environmental Protection Agency, *Economic Impact Analysis*, pp. E5-E15, and Wiseman, *An Introduction to Industrial Organic Chemistry*.

65. John Stille, *Industrial Organic Chemistry* (Englewood Cliffs, N.J.: Prentice-Hall, 1968), p. 74.

66. A list of typical raw materials that can be used in producing furfural, and the pentosan content of each, is found in Heinz K. Krivaneo, *Manufacturing Guide on Furfural* (Paris: United Nations Industrial Development Organization, 1974), p. 33.

67. Rosemary F. Bradley, "Furfural," in *Chemical Economics Handbook* (1978), pp. 583.4601D-583.4601M.

68. Ibid., pp. 583.4601A-583.4601B; W. J. McKillip and E. Sherman, "Furan Derivatives," in *Kirk-Othmer Encyclopedia of Chemical Technology*, 3rd ed., vol. 11, (New York: Wiley-Interscience, 1980), pp. 505-6; and M. V. Sargent and T. M. Crisp, "Furans," in D. Barton and W. D. Ollis, eds., *Comprehensive Organic Chemistry: The Synthesis and Reaction of Organic Compounds*, vol. 4 (Oxford: Pergamon Press, 1979), pp. 693-744.

69. McKillip and Sherman, "Furan Derivatives," p. 506.

70. Marshall Sittig, *Hazardous and Toxic Effects of Industrial Chemicals* (Park Ridge, N.J.: Noyes Data Corp., 1979), pp. 231-32.

71. Bradley, "Furfural," p. 583.4601B.

72. This estimate is derived from ibid., p. 583.4601C, and a comparison of U.S. consumption and import figures.

73. The annual capacity of the Gulf and Western plant at La Romana, Dominican Republic, was approximately 36,300 metric tons in 1980. The only

other plant in the world of similar size is the Quaker Oats plant in Belle Glade, Florida, with an estimated capacity of 32,700 metric tons per year. Ibid., p. 583.4601R.

74. Ibid. 583.4601N.

75. Ibid.

76. Ibid., pp. 583.4601N-583.4601O.

77. Gulf and Western's plant in the Dominican Republic sent substantial amounts of furfural to the United States from 1955 to 1968. Indeed, between 1957 and 1967, imports averaged 28.5 million pounds per annum. Almost all of this was sent from the Gulf and Western plant to a du Pont tetrahydrofuran plant in Niagara Falls, New York. Imports ceased when du Pont closed that plant in 1969. Ibid., 583.4601P.

78. McKillip and Sherman, "Furan Derivatives," p. 507.

79. Krivaneo, *Manufacturing Guide on Furfural*, and International Trade Center, *Making and Marketing Furfural: Added Value for Agro-Industrial Wastes* (Geneva: United Nations Conference on Technology and Development, 1979).

80. McKillip and Sherman, "Furan Derivatives," p. 507.

81. Bradley, "Furfural." p. 583.4601Q.

82. Ibid.

83. McKillip and Sherman, "Furan Derivatives," p. 507.

84. Ibid., pp. 583.4601Q-583.4601U.

85. Dorothy Treskon, "Carbon Black," in *Chemical Economics Handbook* (1978), pp. 731.3000A-731.30001G.

86. "Carbon Black and the Environment," *Rubber Age*, April 1976, pp. 37-42.

87. Treskon, "Carbon Black," p. 731.3000C.

88. Ibid., p. 731.3000M.

89. Chemical and Engineering News, "Carbon Black," *Key Chemicals and Polymers*, 4th ed. (Washington, D.C.: Chemical and Engineering News, 1981), p. 8.

90. U.S. Bureau of the Census, *U.S. Imports for Consumption and General Imports*, Product no. 4730400; and Treskon, "Carbon Black," pp. 731.3001B-731.3001E.

91. "Carbon Black Coloring Banned in Foods, Drugs and Cosmetics; Red No. 4 Use Curbed," *The Wall Street Journal*, September 23, 1976, p. 6.

92. Chemical and Engineering News, "Carbon Black."

93. See U.S. International Trade Commission, *Synthetic Organic Chemicals: U.S. Production and Sales, 1982* (Washington, D.C.: U.S. Government Printing Office, 1983), p. 25.

94. See U.S. Environmental Protection Agency, Office of Research and Development, *Environmental Outlook 1980* (Washington, D.C.: U.S. Government Printing Office, 1980), pp. 612-16.

95. Figures are from Chemical and Engineering News, "Butadiene," *Key Chemicals and Polymers*, p. 7. Information on butadiene production processes supplied by David Blank, Office of Chemicals, U.S. Department of Commerce, in written comments, May 7, 1984.

96. U.S. Department of Health and Human Services, Public Health Service, *Third Annual Report on Carcinogens: Summary* (Washington, D.C.: U.S. Govern-

ment Printing Office, 1983), p. 123.

97. Ibid.

98. Ibid.

99. U.S. Bureau of the Census, *U.S. Imports for Consumption and General Imports*, Product no. 4253660.

100. U.S. Environmental Protection Agency, *Potentially Toxic and Hazardous Substances*, p. iv.

101. A 1982 listing of the manufacturers of about 1,000 cyclic intermediates, for example, shows that well over half are produced by only one company.

102. Based on estimates made by comparison of U.S. import figures for benzenoid intermediate chemicals in U.S. International Trade Commission, *Imports of Benzenoid Chemicals and Products 1982* (Washington, D.C.: U.S. Government Printing Office, 1983) with U.S. production figures for cyclic intermediates in U.S. International Trade Commisssion, *Synthetic Organic Chemicals, 1982.*

103. U.S. International Trade Commission, *Synthetic Organic Chemicals, 1982.*

104. See U.S. Environmental Protection Agency, *Economic Impact Analysis*, pp. E-208 to E-217.

105. U.S. Department of Commerce, *U.S. Industrial Outlook 1980*, p. 125.

106. U.S. Environmental Protection Agency, *Economic Impact Analysis*, p. E-217, and U.S. International Trade Commission, *Imports of Benzenoid Chemicals and Products 1982*, pp. 3-5.

107. U.S. Consumer Product Safety Commission, "Briefing Package on Benzidine Congener Dyes," September 24, 1980.

108. Abbie I. Gerber, Joseph Wagoner, and Peter F. Infante, "Industrial Production and Use Patterns of Benzidine and Benzidine-Based Dyes: Past, Present and Future" (Paper presented at the International Conference on Exportation of Hazardous Industries to Developing Countries, New York, sponsored by the New Directions Program of the University of Connecticut Health Center, November 2-3, 1979), pp. 1-5.

109. U.S. Consumer Product Safety Commission, "Supplemental Briefing Package and Remedial Options Analysis: Petition (CP 79-1) of the Artists-Craftsmen of New York to Ban Selected Products which Contain Benzidine Dyes, O-Tolidine Dyes and O-Dianisidine Dyes," September 24, 1980, pp. 2-3.

110. Arthur R. Gregory, "Carcinogenicity of Benzidine, O-Tolidine and O-Dianisidine and Dyes Made From These Substances," contained in U.S. Consumer Product Safety Commission, "Supplemental Briefing Package."

111. Marilyn Wind, "Metabolism of Benzidine, O-Tolidine,and O-Dianisidine Based Dyes," contained in U.S. Consumer Product Safety Commission, "Supplemental Briefing Package."

112. U.S. Department of Health, Education, and Welfare, National Institute for Occupational Safety and Health; and National Cancer Institute, *Current Intelligence Bulletin 24*, April 17, 1978.

113. U.S. Department of Labor, Occupational Safety and Health Administration, and U.S. Department of Health and Human Services, National Institute for Occupational Safety and Health, "Benzidine, o-Tolidine-, and o-Dianisidine-Based Dyes: Health Hazard Alert," Department of Health and Human Services (NIOSH) Publication no. 81-106, December 1980.

114. JRB Associates, "Survey of the Manufacture, Import, and Uses for Benzidine, Related Substances, and Related Dyes and Pigments" (Report submitted to U.S. Environmental Protection Agency, Office of Toxic Substances, Contract no. 68-81-5105, May 23, 1979), p. 4-1.

115. Ibid., p. 61.

116. See ibid., p. 6-34, table 6.5, for a list of these firms.

117. For example, all but one of NIOSH's list of 42 commercially important benzidine-related dyes are direct dyes. Of 112 benzidine-related dyes no longer produced in the United States, 108 are direct dyes. See ibid., p. 6-5, and pp. 6-8 to 6-11, table 6-2.

118. Calculated from data in U.S. International Trade Commission, *Imports of Benzenoid Chemicals and Products*, 1973-82 annual editions.

119. Calculated from import data in ibid., and U.S. production data contained in U.S. International Trade Commission, *Synthetic Organic Chemicals*, 1977-82 annual editions.

120. Although their share has declined from 97 percent in 1973, West Germany, Japan, Switzerland, the United Kingdom, and France still accounted for 88 percent of the total value of U.S. benzedine-dye imports in 1982. Notably, however, Japan's share of total import value grew from about 2 percent in 1973 total import value to 25 percent in 1982. U.S. International Trade Commission, *Imports of Benzenoid Chemicals and Products 1982*, p. 35.

121. Ibid.

122. See Cate Jenkins, "Benzidine, o-Tolidine, o-Dianisidine, and Their Derivative Dyes: Technical Control and Options Analysis" (Draft report of U.S. Environmental Protection Agency, Office of Pesticides and Toxic Substances, August 21, 1980).

123. Information provided to the author by officials of the Romanian Ministry of the Chemical Industry in an interview conducted in Bucharest, Romania, on July 9, 1980. The officials were: Paul G. Mgravescu, general inspector; John Tiberiu Hudea, chief of Fertilizer Department; John Mandravel, engineer in the Petrochemical Department; Corneliu Craiu, technical director of the Research and Design Institute for Wastewater Treatment; and Pavel Mariana, engineer.

124. McRae, Whelchel and Rowland, eds., *Toxic Substances Control Sourcebook*, p. 86.

125. U.S. Department of Commerce, *U.S. Industrial Outlook 1981*, p. 147.

126. Stanford Research Institute, "Pesticide Industry Overview," in *Chemical Economics Handbook* (1980), p. 573.1000D

127. Ibid.

128. Ibid.

129. For an excellent overview of this topic see Ruth Norris et. al., *Pills, Pesticides and Profits: The International Trade in Toxic Substances* (Croton-on-Hudson, N.Y.: North River Press, 1982).

130. Ibid., pp. 7-8.

131. U.S. Environmental Protection Agency, *Environmental Outlook 1980* (Washington, D.C.: U.S. Government Printing Office, 1980), p. 620.

132. Stanford Research Institute, "Pesticide Industry Overview," pp. 573.1003G-573.1003R.

133. Ibid., pp. 573.1001B.

134. Calculated from U.S. International Trade Commission, *Synthetic Organic Chemicals 1982*, p. 225.

135. Calculated from figures in ibid. and U.S. International Trade Commission, *Imports of Benzenoid Chemicals and Products 1982*, p. 97.

136. Calculated from sources cited in n. 135.

137. Stanford Research Institute, "Pesticide Industry Overview," p. 573.1001I.

138. Ibid., pp. 573.1001G,H.

139. U.S. International Trade Commission, *Synthetic Organic Chemicals: U.S. Production and Sales, 1978* (Washington, D.C.: U.S. Government Printing Office, 1979), p. 273.

140. Stanford Research Institute, "Insecticides," in *Chemical Economics Handbook* (1979), pp. 573.3005V-573.3005Y.

141. Stanford Research Institute, "Pesticide Industry Overview," p. 573.1001L.

142. Stanford Research Institute, "Herbicides," in *Chemical Economics Handbook* (1980), pp. 573.7009Y-573.710A.

143. Stanford Research Institute, "Pesticide Industry Overview," pp. 573.1000C, 573.1001F, and 573.1001L.

144. Ibid., p. 573.1003A.

145. U.S. International Trade Commission, *Synthetic Organic Chemicals 1978*, p. 273.

146. U.S. Department of Health and Human Services, Public Health Service, *Second Annual Report on Carcinogens* (Washington, D.C.: U.S. Government Printing Office, 1981), pp. 152-53.

147. Ibid.

148. Stanford Research Institute, "Fumigants and Nematicides," in *Chemical Economics Handbook* (1983), p. 573.9006O.

149. Ibid., p. 573.9007E.

150. Ronald B. Taylor, "Production of Highly Toxic Pesticide Shifts to Mexico," *Los Angeles Times*, September 9, 1978, sec. II, p. 1.

151. Ibid. See also Stanford Research Institute, "Fumigants and Nematicides," pp. 573.9007E and 573.9007Q.

152. Stanford Research Institute, "Fumigants and Nematicides," pp. 573.9007E and 573.9007Q.

153. Ibid., p. 573.9006J.

154. Chris Jenkins, "DBCP: A Runaway Hazard," *NACLA Report* 12, no. 2 (March-April 1979):43-45.

155. Andy Pasztor, "EPA Moves Against Dicofol, Contends Widely Used Insecticide Contains DDT," *Wall Street Journal*, March 19, 1984.

5. Planning for the Future

The research presented in this report indicates that neither the costs nor the logistics of complying with environmental regulations are emerging as decisive across-the-board factors inducing U.S. manufacturing industries to construct more branch plants overseas rather than in the United States. To the extent that a long-term process of "redeployment" by a broad range of industries away from the United States to less-industrialized countries is occurring, there is no evidence that environmental factors have increased the trend to any significant degree for the vast majority of U.S. industries. Indeed, overall foreign investments and U.S. imports have increased faster among the manufacturing industries with low pollution-control costs than they have among those that have borne the major burdens of environmental and workplace-health regulations—mineral-processing, chemical, and pulp and paper companies.

This finding does not mean that environmental regulations have not burdened U.S. companies in high-pollution industrial sectors. Nor does it mean that environmental regulations are not important in the industrial-location process. It means that even if the differentials in the cost of complying with environmental regulations in industrialized and industrializing countries are influential, they have not been strong enough to offset larger trends shaping aggregate international industrial-siting patterns. Government policy makers should keep this finding in mind as they consider whether to weaken, maintain, or strengthen existing environmental regulations and as they study ways to encourage renewed industrial expansion in the United States.

INDUSTRY-BY-INDUSTRY EFFECTS OF ENVIRONMENTAL REGULATIONS

Only a relatively small number of U.S. industries appear to have had their international-location patterns significantly affected by environmental regulations in the United States. Instead, most industries that have been hard hit by those regulations have been able to adapt to them by changing their production processes or by using different raw materials. Even when these adaptations have not reduced regulatory burdens, the environmental problems generally have not been substantial enough to offset factors that more traditionally have determined how most firms select foreign locations for branch-plant construction (for example, market considerations, transportion, raw-material availability, labor costs, and political stability). Only in industries where demand has been stagnant or declining, or where no significant technological breakthroughs can be envisioned to reduce environment-related hazards, are there significant examples of the production of a product being increasingly transferred overseas.

High-Growth Industries Not Pushed Overseas

No significant examples of industrial flight exist among industries where demand is expanding and U.S. producers are enjoying technological superiority. Relocation of an industrial facility abroad has been only one of a number of possible responses for these high-growth firms as they have faced growing regulatory costs and environmental restrictions. Technological innovation, use of new raw materials or substitute products, reclamation of waste materials, tighter process and quality controls, and other adaptations generally have proven better responses than flight for many industries. Transportation costs, domestic availability of raw materials, uniform product standards that apply to all products on the U.S. market (whether they are produced in the United States or abroad), and other factors have made it difficult to leave the United States, even when environment-related problems have been formidable.

The industries producing polyvinyl chloride (PVC) and acrylonitrile are two notable examples where intense regulatory pressures and adverse publicity have not prompted significant movements by U.S. producers to other countries. U.S. producers of PVC have remained highly competitive despite heavy restrictions caused by concern that exposure to its basic component, vinyl chloride monomer, could lead to angiosarcoma, a rare cancer of the liver. PVC is the second largest volume thermoplastic produced, and demand for it, especially in making plastic pipes and other products related to the construction industry, has increased rapidly over the last 15 years.

PVC resin is produced by polymerizing vinyl chloride monomer. Exposure to the monomer in its raw form, as an atmospheric emission, or as a residual in PVC products all appear to cause angiosarcoma. As a result, PVC manufacturers have had to make large capital and operating expenditures to reduce exposure to the monomer at all stages of production and use. This has included developing manufacturing processes to comply with stringent standards that cover the amount of vinyl chloride monomer that can exist in the workplace, be contained in plant emissions, or remain as an impurity in PVC resins.

In spite of decreased construction activity since the late 1970s, most U.S. manufacturers have been able to absorb these costs because of rapidly escalating demand for PVC products. The technology to achieve the necessary reductions was available when it was needed, so U.S. producers did not face major pressures to relocate in less-regulated countries to maintain production. In addition, even though PVC production has increased greatly in Europe and several rapidly industrializing countries, the U.S. standard requiring PVC resin to contain fewer than 5 parts per million of residual vinyl chloride monomer has blocked an influx of low-cost, low-quality PVC to challenge the higher-cost PVC of U.S. producers.

The case of acrylonitrile is almost identical to that of PVC. U.S. producers in both instances have remained strong, even though the two chemicals are produced by major chemical firms that operate worldwide and have not had their mobility hampered by locational factors such as raw-material availability or transportation costs. Ultimately, the rapid expansion of domestic demand for these two chemicals and the concomitant incentives to invest in new technological developments have given these industries large cushions to weather the onslaught of new regulations and public concern.

A Few Industries Affected

Although most U.S. manufacturing industries have adapted to stringent environmental regulations without relocating plants abroad, international-locational trends in some industries do appear to have been either influenced or determined by these regulations. For a variety of reasons, the importance of environmental factors has been elevated in the location decisions made by some of the industries studied in chapters 3 and 4.

Environmental Regulation as a Cocatalyst

In several industries, environmental regulations have interacted with a wide variety of other economic and regulatory trends to reinforce an already-existing propensity to locate manufacturing facilities overseas. The importance of this cocatalyst role varies among the different industries examined.

Environmental regulations also appear to have increased, at least slightly, the trend toward worldwide purchasing of intermediate organic chemicals. Whole industries have not necessarily fled the United States, but large U.S. chemical companies apparently have been going abroad to produce or purchase a few intermediates needed for chemical production within the United States. This appears to have been the case for butadiene, thiourea, and several dozen low-volume intermediates in the benzenoid group. However, assessing how influential environmental considerations have become in any given instance is difficult for several reasons: world trade in intermediate organic chemicals would have grown rapidly even without workplace-health and antipollution regulations; many large chemical companies have increasingly sought to build large facilities to supply their regional or even worldwide demand for certain intermediates; and a large percentage of international trade in intermediates takes place as intracompany transfers across borders.

Environmental Regulation as a Primary Location Factor

For a few industries, pollution and workplace-health standards have indeed become the primary causes of production declining in the United States and increasing overseas. In particular, U.S. production of asbestos, arsenic trioxide, benzidine-based dyes, certain pesticides, and a few known carcinogenic chemicals has been disrupted or halted by strict regulations and growing public awareness of the dangers of these substances. In cases where domestic demand for these products has not declined as quickly as has domestic production, some U.S. companies have moved to produce these substances abroad, importing them or products derived from them into the United States. Other U.S. companies have purchased these substances from foreign producers.

Often, however, this has proven to be a temporary situation, since consumption, as well as production, of hazardous substances tends to be restricted or banned. Most benzidine-based dyes and the pesticides lindane, DBCP, and dicofol are examples of products whose U.S. imports rose after regulations and public concern disrupted U.S. production, only to stop or decline dramatically when the uses of the substances were halted or severely curtailed.

Characteristics of Affected Industries

The widely divergent responses of industries with similar pollution and workplace-safety problems to changing environmental regulations underlines the fact that some industries are more susceptible than others to these regulations and have fewer choices other than to move abroad. The cases of PVC and acrylonitrile help to emphasize that two of the most significant variables affecting how an industry responds to intense regulatory pressures and public concern appear to be long-term domestic demand and technological outlook. If demand for a product is forecast to remain strong despite environmental problems, and if technological gains appear possible through research and development, overseas flight is unlikely. However, U.S. firms are more likely to respond to strict environmental standards by relocating productive facilities overseas, if:

- Complying with U.S. environmental regulations is impeded not only by financial costs but also because a pollution or workplace-safety problem is so acute that it is difficult to ensure safety even with large infusions of capital for new technology.
- The regulations inhibit a product's production (for example, by governing workplace health) more than its final consumption, so that the problems associated with the product can be "left behind" in a new producing country.
- The regulations and procedures, as well as local opposition and lengthy public participation, have severely limited the number of sites where new facilities for an industry may be located.
- Demand for the product is relatively inelastic—that is, substitute raw materials, intermediates, and final products are unavailable or uneconomical, and, even though the product cannot be produced in the United States, it is essential to some consumer sector or industry.
- Production tends to be labor-intensive rather than capital-intensive, decreasing the likelihood that all environmental and safety difficulties can be solved with technological innovation or closed production processes that do not expose workers to problem substances.
- Shipping costs are low relative to production costs and the weight and volume of the product.

Taken together, these characteristics indicate that industries are most likely to move abroad to avoid environmental regulations if they either are manufacturing products for which consumption is irreversibly declining or are at an advanced stage of the international product cycle where competitiveness is determined more by direct production and shipping costs than by possession of a superior product or a technological advantage in production.

Often, as has already been noted, the movement to production facilities or purchasing abroad takes place in the period between the introduction of new regulations and the discovery of substitute products or new technologies. In some cases, this period may be relatively brief, but, in other cases, the interregnum may be rather lengthy, as it has been in the asbestos industry. Asbestos has proven to be a difficult product to replace because of its frictional, heat-resistance, and binding qualities; adequate substitutes are only slowly being developed. Thus, while major asbestos companies such as Johns-Manville and Raybestos Manhattan have vowed to move as rapidly as possible to nonasbestos product lines and have reduced asbestos product manufacturing in the United States, they have been relying increasingly on supplies from their foreign subsidiaries and other overseas producers until a replacement for asbestos is available.

The position of individual companies within their own industries—their financial state, the technologies they employ, the products they manufacture in conjunction with others at the same site, their relationship with overseas producers, and sources of raw materials—can also lead them to adopt a strategy of relocation abroad even when other firms do not. In some industries (for example, cement and titanium dioxide), a few companies have reacted to environmental regulations and other forces shaping their domestic outlook by moving their operations abroad or by getting out of the industry, while other established producers or new entrants into the same industry have made substantial new investments—increasing productive capacity and decreasing pollution problems at the same time.

This phenomenon underlines two important points: (a) often, individual company responses to new environmental regulations have been based as much on the personal outlooks of key corporate decision makers as on objective analysis of the long-term profit potential within an industry; and (b) some companies within certain industries have found themselves particularly vulnerable to new regulations. Sometimes this has been due to poor decisions that a company made about technology, location, or governmental commitment to pollution-control regulations. In other cases, the new regulations and economic fluctuations of the 1970s caught a company just after it had built new industrial facilities and forced it to make large additional investments in pollution control.

POLICY IMPLICATIONS

Since most industries that have responded to environmental regulations by transferring production overseas no longer are dynamic forces within the U.S. economy, their exoduses are not likely to have major deleterious effects on the United States's economy or overall industrial base. Localized economic and employment disruptions are likely as these industries continue to decline, but, on a national basis, most of them will gradually be replaced as cleaner, safer products that utilize more technologically advanced manufacturing processes are developed. More and more substitutes for harmful dyes, arsenic, highly toxic pesticides, and even asbestos are being, and will continue to be, introduced. Gradually, these new products (or, alternatively, more advanced technologies for production and use of existing products) will absorb most of the intermediate and end-product uses for these hazardous minerals and chemicals. Relief from the workplace-health, pollution, and consumer-safety standards that are speeding the obsolescence of hazardous industrial materials would, therefore, not just increase worker- and public-health hazards. It would also remove an important incentive for technological progress.

General Trends

Nevertheless, several of the trends noted in this report may, if they continue over time, have a growing significance for the U.S. economy and the overall outlook for manufacturing industries. In addition, policy makers may have to be concerned about the welfare of those workers who do lose their jobs as a result of movement abroad related to the stringency of environmental regulations, even though the total relative number of industries and workers affected will remain small. The trends that may provoke the greatest policy debates in the future are summarized below.

Declining Hazardous Industries

Only one trend—the flight of certain hazardous industries that are declining because of the combination of environmental regulations and extreme concern by workers and the public about the hazards in these industries—is directly attributable to environmental regulations and concern in the United States. Although environmental regulations may, in effect, be killing these industries, the answer clearly is not to resurrect them through regulatory relief. None of the products affected by this trend are of essential economic or strategic importance. In most cases, new, safer substitutes are being introduced in their place.

A moral case might be made that the United States should ban the importation of products whose production we are unwilling to tolerate and should prohibit U.S. firms in these industries from moving abroad to continue producing at the expense of foreign workers. But such a suggestion would invite trade retaliation and be viewed as unfair by foreign competitors. In addition, from a public-policy perspective, the proposal would be difficult to develop and administer. How, for example, would the federal government react toward a new pesticide developed overseas and not yet produced in the United States? Domestic firms seeking to keep the product out of the U.S. market might argue that they do not produce it because of the environmental hazards involved. Short of an outright ban on the use and production of certain substances, it would be difficult to screen imports according to criteria pertaining to the circumstances under which they were produced.

Still, whether or not domestic use of a product is banned, the U.S. government does have some responsibility when declining dangerous industries in the United States stimulate increased production abroad. For example, the government has a legitimate role to play in encouraging the research and development process within such industries to help them find and commercialize cleaner, safer, and higher quality substitute products. Moreover, the government should not assist the industrial-flight efforts of such industries by approving loans, tax credits, or risk-sharing arrangements through the Overseas Private Investment Corporation, the Export-Import Bank, or any other government agency. The reasons are economic and political as well as moral. In the long term, offshore investments in such products will prove to be counterproductive, since substitutes will replace them or they will be banned outright for consumption as well as use. For individual companies, incentives available from the U.S. government could turn a bad-risk into a no-risk situation, but they would not change the objective situation. And when people in a country that has accepted a company with environmental or workplace hazards begin to resent its presence, they may remember first and foremost that it is a U.S. firm backed by the U.S. government.

Mineral Processing

The potential international-location impacts of environmental factors in mineral-processing industries may also deserve the attention of U.S. policy makers. In the cases of copper, zinc, and lead, the U.S. industrial economy clearly must maintain a certain level of domestic ore-processing capacity. Although it will be increasingly difficult to find countries willing to allow unprocessed ores from their mines to be sent to the United States, it should be a goal of U.S. policy at least to continue the domestic processing of ores that are mined within the United States.

As has been discussed in chapter 3, relief from environmental regulations probably could not, on its own, reverse the declines of U.S. mineral producers. Policy solutions to assist key mineral-processing industries should look toward technological innovation, rather than seek to roll back regulations that clearly have enormous public-health implications. In the long term, the U.S. mineral-processing industries will remain competitive in world production circles only if they move their U.S. manufacturing facilities nearer to markets for sulfuric acid and for processed minerals, alter their technologies, and become more energy-efficient. Extensive regulatory relief would only perpetuate the status quo and delay much needed advancements in these areas.

Intermediate Chemicals

Finally, environmental regulations and concern may have broad locational impacts in the future in the vast realm of intermediate-organic-chemical production. Large-quantity intermediates as well as thousands of small-quantity ones are increasingly being produced in one country for use in the manufacturing of final goods in other countries.

In recent years, U.S. imports of many intermediates have been on the rise, and some of these chemicals have faced intense regulatory scrutiny. It is impossible to say, however, whether these trends will become more pronounced in the future and, if so, how important the role of environmental regulations will be. The best public-policy response for now is to continue monitoring trends as they develop in the 1980s.

An Integrative Approach

On the whole, then, the contention that U.S. environmental regulations should be relaxed because they have contributed to widespread movement overseas by U.S. industries cannot be substantiated. Any effort within Congress or the executive branch to roll back, weaken, or fail to enforce existing environmental regulations cannot legitimately be supported by arguing that the stringency of those regulations has caused a significant amount of the United States' productive capacity in manufacturing industries to be transferred abroad.

Across-the-board policy approaches to the problems of industrial relocation—either restrictions on relocations or sweeping regulatory relief—are unnecessary, unwise, and unfeasible. Instead, what is needed to solve the particular industrial-relocation problems noted in this report is some effort to ensure that environmental regulations do not work at cross-purposes with emerging government policies aimed at bringing about long-term technological progress and structural change within specific industries. Environmental policies must be viewed much more integrally as part of the whole bundle of governmental policies that seek to enhance and reward the growth industries of the future and to cushion the hardships wrought when old industrial sectors begin to decline.

From a policy perspective, the United States should be *more* concerned if environmental regulations drive otherwise healthy industries from its shores or increase foreign dependence within essential sectors of the industrial economy. But rolling back environmental regulations where they speed the decline of obsolescent industries will almost certainly be counterproductive for the long-term goal of strong U.S. industrial growth through technological innovation.

Index

Acetic acid, 105
Acetylene, 98
Acrylonitrile, 105, 133
Africa, 48
Aldrin, 118
Alkalies, 83
Allied Chemical, 87
Alumina, 86, 87
Aluminum fluoride, 87
Aluminum hydroxide, 86
Ammonia, 83
AMVAC, 122
Aromatic amines, synthetic,
113
Arsenic trioxide
effect of regulation on,
production, 5
imports of, 60, *61*
industry trends, 59-63
production of, *61*
production processes of,
60-63
recovery of, in smelting
process, 59-60
uses of, 59
Asarco, 48, 60, 62, 63
Asbestos, 136
effect of environmental and
safety regulations on,
production, 5, 63-70
human health hazards of,
64-65
imports of, goods by U.S.,
68, 69
industry trends, 65-70
maquiladors operations of,
66, 67n
as substitute for slab zinc,
53-54
uses of, 65
Asbestosis, 64
Australia, 44, 48, 56

Balance of trade. *See* Exports;
Imports
BASF, 120
Belgium, 92, 109
Bentazon, 120
Benzene, 98
Benzenoids, 134
carcinogenicity of, 109
imports of, by U.S., 109-
112, 118-120, *111*, *119*
use of, in pesticides, 118-120
Benzidine-based dyes. *See*
Dyes, benzidine-based
Blast furnace, 50
Boric acid, 83
Boston Consulting Group, 73
Brazil, 95, 103
Brookings Institution, the, 15
Bureau of Mines, 47, 62, 71,
74
Bush, George, 9
Business Policy Analysis,
Office of (DOC), 47
Butadiene, 105, 107, 134, *108*

Canada, 33, 48, 66, 75, 87,
93, 98, 112, *68, 69*
Capital expenditures. *See* Expenditures; Investments
Carbon black
imports of, to U.S., *106*
pollution caused by processing of, 104
production processes for,
104
uses of, 103
Carter administration, 8, 9, 47
Castleman, Barry, 5
Castleman report, 5, 9, 17-18
Cement, 63, 136
effect of environmental and
safety regulations on,
industry, 71-73
imports of, by U.S., 72

industry trends, 70-71,
73-75, 77
production process of, 71,
73-75
technological innovations
by, industry, 74-75
Central America, 122
Chemical industry, 3
capital expenditures by
foreign affiliates of U.S.,
24, 26
capital expenditures of, in
LDCs, 31-33, 32
expenditures by, for pollution control, 18, 20
foreign investments by,
30-31
future policy for, 139
imports by, 25-28, 34
imports of, goods by U.S.,
27, 28
investment in foreign, by
U.S. companies, 23
and U.S. economy, 83
see also Inorganic chemical
processors; Organic chemical processors
Chemical Manufacturers
Association, 1
Chemicals
exports of, by foreign
affiliates of U.S. com-
panies, 29, 30
as a high-pollution industry,
17
imports to U.S. of, from
LDCs, 34
inorganic. See Inorganic
chemicals
organic. See Organic
chemicals
U.S. imports of, 27, 28
Chile, 48
China, 103

Chlordimeform, 120
Chlorine, 84
Cities Service Company, 104
Clean Air Act, 7, 10, 44, 64
Clean Water Act, 58
Clinker. See Cement
Colombia, 121
Copper
and arsenic trioxide by-
product, 59-60
effect of environmental and
safety regulations on,
industry, 45-48
export of, by LDCs, 46
furnace technology of,
industry, 50-51
import quotas for foreign,
47
imports of, to U.S., 46
industry trends, 45, 49, 77
pollutants from smelting of,
45
production process of, 47-50
Commerce Department. See
Department of Commerce,
U.S.
Consumer Product Safety
Commission, 64
Costs
of plant and equipment. See
Expenditures; Investments
of pollution control. See
Expenditures; Investments
of production. See
Expenditures
of transportation. See
Investments; Production
of workplace health and
safety. See Expenditures
Council of Economic Advisers,
8
Crandall, Robert W., 15
Cryolite, 87
Cyclohexane, 105

DBCP, 122-123
DDT, 118, 123
DeMuth, Christopher, 15
Department of Commerce,
    U.S., 25, 36, 47, 48, 51,
    58, 66, 92, 97, 107, 112
Department of Health and
    Human Services, U.S.,
    107
Department of the Treasury,
    U.S., 90-92
Developing countries. *See*
    LDCs
Dicofol, 123
Dieldrin, 118
Dioxin, 121
Diuron, 120-121
Dominican Republic, 100, 103
Dow Chemical, 121
Duerksen, Christopher J., 4
du Pont, 87, 92-93, 121
Dyes, benzidine-based
    human health effects of,
        113-114
    imports of, related to ban,
        115-117
    production of, 114-115
    synthetic aromatic amines
        in, 113
    uses of, 113
Dyes, direct, 114-115, *116*

EDB, 122
Egypt, 115
Eli Lilly, 121
England, 120
Environmental policy. *See*
    Policy
Environmental Protection
    Agency, U.S., 4, 48, 56,
    58, 64, 96, 104, 109, 112,
    117n, 121, 122-123

Environmental regulations
    air-pollution offsets, 4
    attempts to devise, for
        organic chemical industry,
        95-97
    as cocatalyst in locational
        decisions, 133-134
    and demand for lead, 56-58
    effect of, on arsenic trioxide
        production, 59-63
    effect of, on benzenoid pes-
        ticide producers, 118-120
    effect of, on benzidine-based
        dye producers, 113-117
    effect of, on carbon black
        processors, 105
    effect of, on cement in-
        dustry, 71, 73
    effect of, on chemical in-
        dustry, 83-123
    effect of, on foreign invest-
        ment trends, 21-33
    effect of, on furfural pro-
        duction, 102-103
    effect of, on lead industry,
        55-59
    effect of, on pesticide pro-
        ducers, 118-123
    effect of, on metal proces-
        sors, 42-63
    effect of, on nonmetallic-
        mineral processors, 63-76
    effect of, on thiourea in-
        dustry, 107-109
    effect of, on U.S. copper
        industry, 45-48
    effect of, on U.S. import
        trends, 21-33
    effect of, on zinc processors,
        51-55
    future policy for, 131-140
    and industrial-flight hypoth-
        esis, 2-5, 9-10, 17-20

industries affected by,
133-136
industry-by-industry effects
of, 131-137
permitting processes of, 9-10
prevention of significant
deterioration, 4
as primary locational factor,
134-136
relaxing of, 7, 44, 138-139,
140
relief from, 137
undermining intent of, by
U.S. corporations, 6
EPA *See* Environmental Protection Agency, U.S.
Europe, Eastern, 56, 103, 121
Europe, Western, 42, 48-49,
50, 56, 92, 94, 98, 103,
104, 112, 115, 120, 121
European Economic Commu-
nity, 94
Ethylbenzene, 105
Ethylenes, 98, 105
Expenditures
as cause of industrial relocation, 9-10
by chemical industry for
pollution control, 84-85, *18*
by metal processors for
pollution control, 43-44, *18*
by petroleum industry for
pollution control, *18*
for pollution control by all
manufacturing, *18, 20*
for pollution control by
pollution-intensive in-
dustries, *18, 19, 20*
by pulp and paper industry
for pollution control, *18*
see also Investments
Export-Import Ban, 138
Exports
of asbestos goods by LDCs
to U.S., *68, 69*

of carbon black by U.S.,
104
of chemicals to U.S., *29, 30*
of copper to U.S., *46*
by foreign affiliates of U.S.
companies to U.S., *29, 30*
of furfural from LDCs,
102-103
of high-volume intermediate
organic chemicals by U.S.,
107
of lead, *57*
of pesticides by U.S., 117-
118, 117n
of processed minerals to
U.S., *29, 30*
see also Imports

FDA. *See* Food and Drug Administration, U.S.
Finland, 99
Fluorspar. *See* Hydrofluoric
acid
Food and Drug Administra-
tion, U.S., 105
France, 60, 63, 92, 99
Frasch process, 50
Fungicides. *See* Pesticides
Furfural
effects of environmental regulation on, industry, 99
imports of, by U.S., *101*
pollution caused by processing of, 100
production of, 100-103
production processes for,
99-100
uses of, 99
Furnace technology, 50-51,
53-54

General Accounting Office, 43
General Agreement on Tariffs
and Trade, 75

Germany, Federal Republic of, 44, 92, 93, 109
Gladwin, Thomas, 4, 17
Gold, 59
Gulf and Western Industries, 53, 100-103
Gypsum, 63, 86

Hawaii, 122
Health concerns. *See* Public opinion
Health and Human Services, Department of. *See* Department of Health and Human Services, U.S.
Health standards. *See* Environmental regulations
Herbicides. *See* Pesticides
High-pollution industries. *See* Industry, pollution-intensive
Horizontal retort furnace, 53-54
Hydrocarbons. *See* Organic chemicals
Hydrochloric acid, 83, 86
Hydrofluoric acid
  demand for, 87
  factors affecting international trade of, 89-90
  imports of, to U.S., 86-87, 88
  pollution from processing of, 86
  production of, in U.S., 88
  production processes for, 86
  uses of, 87-88
Hydrometallurgical reduction, 53

Imports
  of arsenic trioxide by U.S., 60, 61, 62-63
of asbestos by U.S., 66, 68, 69
of benzenoid pesticides by U.S., 118-120, 119
of benzenoids by U.S., 109-112, 111
of benzedine-based dyes by U.S., 115-117
of butadiene by U.S., 107, 108
of carbon black by U.S., 105, 106
of cement by U.S., 73, 72
of chemicals by U.S., 27, 28, 34
of copper by U.S., 46
of direct dyes by U.S., 115, 116
of furfural by U.S., 100-102, 101
of high-volume intermediate organic chemicals by U.S., 107
of hydrofluoric acid by U.S., 86-87, 88
of lead by U.S., 57
from LDCs by U.S., 33, 34
of low-volume intermediate organic chemicals by U.S., 109
of manufactured goods by U.S., 25-28, 27, 28
of pesticides by U.S., 118-122
of pollution-intensive goods by U.S., 25-28
of processed minerals by U.S., 27, 28, 34
of pulp and paper goods by U.S., 27, 28, 34
quotas of, for copper industry, 47
tariffs on, for hydrofluoric acid, 86

of thiourea by U.S., 109, 110
of titanium dioxide by U.S., 90-93, 91
trends of U.S., 21-33
of zinc by U.S., 52
see also Exports
India, 103, 115
Indonesia, 105
Industrial-flight hypothesis
    and constraints on hazard-ous production, 4-5
    and data inadequacy, 9-10
    explanation of, 2-5
    government response to, 7-9
    and national security, 1-2
    and plant siting, 3-4
    policy implications of, 137-140
    politics of, 6-7
    and pollution-control costs, 2-3
    reactions to prospects of, 6-10
    and transportation costs, 41
Industrial location. See Loca-tion patterns, international
Industrial production. See Production
Industry, manufacturing
    base of, 1
    capital expenditures by, 22-25
    capital expenditures by, in LDCs, 32
    capital expenditures by foreign affiliates of U.S., 24
    effect of shift to service on, 4
    expenditures by, for pollu-tion control, 18, 20
    foreign investments by, 22
    imports to U.S. of, goods, 27, 28, 34

    investment in foreign, by U.S. companies, 23, 31
    see also Industry, pollution-intensive
Industry, pollution-intensive
    capital expenditures by, 22-25
    capital expenditures by foreign affiliates of U.S., 24, 26
    capital expenditures of, in LDCs, 31-33
    chemical, 83-123, 18
    effect of environmental reg-ulations on, by industry, 131-137
    expenditures by, for pollu-tion control, 18, 19, 20
    foreign investment trends of, 21-33
    general trends of, 137-139
    investments in, foreign, by U.S. companies, 23
    investments in LDCs by, 30-31
    locational disruptions of, 33-36
    mineral processing, 41-81, 18
    petroleum, 18
    pulp and paper, 18
    susceptibility of, to reloca-tion, 17-20
    see also Mineral industry; Chemical industry; Petro-leum industry; Pulp and paper industry
Inorganic chemical processors
    effect of environmental and safety standards on, 84-85
    of hydrofluoric acid, 86-90
    industry trends, 85-86
    and research and develop-ment, 84
    of titanium dioxide, 90-94

Inorganic chemicals, 83-94
  alkalies, 83
  alumina, 86
  aluminum hydroxide, 86
  aluminum fluoride, 87
  ammonia, 83
  boric acid, 83
  hydrochloric acid, 83, 86
  hydrofluoric acid, 86-90
  nitric acid, 83
  phosphates, 86
  phosphoric acid, 83
  pollution from, processing, 84
  potassium, 86
  production processes for, 84
  sodium compounds, 86
  sulfuric acid, 83, 86
  titanium dioxide, 83, 90-94
  uranium compounds, 86
  uses of, 83-84
  zinc oxide, 83
  see also Inorganic chemical processors
Insecticides. See Pesticides
Intermediate organic chemicals
  acetic acid, 105
  acrylonitrile, 105
  benzenoids, 109-112, 111
  butadiene, 105, 107, 108
  cyclohexane, 105
  ethylbenzene, 105
  ethylene dichloride, 105
  ethylene glycol, 105
  ethylene oxide, 105
  phenol, 107
  phthalic anhydride, 107
  production of, 107-109
  styrene monomer, 107
  terephthalic acid, 107
  thiourea, 107-109, 134, 110
  vinyl chloride, 105
International Trade Commission, U.S., 47, 92, 93, 100, 109, 112

Investments
  in cement production abroad, 74
  foreign, by all industrial manufacturers, 22
  foreign, by high-pollution industries, 22
  foreign, by U.S. companies, 23
  influences on, for industry, 36
  in LDCs by U.S. companies, 30-31, 31
  trends of foreign, by U.S. pollution-intensive industries, 21-33
  by U.S. manufacturers, 23
  see also Expenditures
Ireland, 44, 67n
Israel, 121
Italy, 114
ITC. See International Trade Commission, U.S.

Japan, 42, 48, 49, 50, 51, 56, 71, 98, 104, 109, 112, 114, 120
Johns-Manville Corporation, 66, 136

Kenya, 103

Latin America, 7
LDCs
  and asbestos industry, 66-67, 67n
  and benzidine-based dye product industry, 115-117
  capital expenditures in, by U.S. companies, 32
  export of asbestos goods by, to U.S., 68, 69

export of furfural by, 102-103
and hydrofluoric acid manufacture, 90
industrial strategies of, 85
investment in, by U.S. companies, 30-31
nationalized industries in, for mineral production, 41
participation of, in copper industry, 49-50
and pesticide production, 121-122
and supply of arsenic trioxide, 60-62
trade with, 28-33
U.S. direct investment in, *31*
and U.S., importations, 21, 33
and zinc industry, 54-55
Lead
and arsenic trioxide by-product, 59
export of, *57*
import of, *57*
industry trends, 55-56
pollutants generated by, processing, 58-59
production of, in U.S., *57*
Lepanto Consolidated Ltd., 63
Less-developed countries. *See* LDCs
Lindane, 121-122
Linuron, 121
Location patterns, international
for acrylonitrile producers, 133
for asbestos industry, 66-70
for benzenoid chemical producers, 112
cocatalyst effects of environmental and safety regulations in, 133-134
effect of environmental regulations on, 4-5

effect of patents on, 121-122
effect of workplace health standards on, 4-5
factors affecting decision making, 134-136
for furfural processing industry, 102-103
general trends of, 137-139
for hydrofluoric acid producers, 89-90
industrial-flight hypothesis, 2-5
for inorganic chemical processors, 85-86
of metal processors, 42-43
of pesticide producers, 121-123
politics of, 6-7
for polyvinyl chloride producers, 132-133
reactions to change in, 6-10
theories governing, 2-3
of thiourea producers, 109
for titanium dioxide manufacturers, 93-94
unaffected, for high-growth industries, 132-133
see also Industrial-flight hypothesis

Market access. *See* Production
Marshall, Ray, 8
Metal processors
and arsenic trioxide by-product, 59-63
of copper, 44-51
expenditures by, for pollution and safety control, 43-44
of lead, 55-59
locational trends of, 42-43
nonmetallic-mineral processors, 63-76
regulatory relief for, 44

of zinc, 51-55
see also Nonmetallic-mineral
  processors
Metals. See Minerals
Methanol, 98
Mexico, 60, 62-63, 66, 67, 87,
  89, 90, 103, 121, 122, *68,
  69*
Milan, Manuel Medellin, 67
Mineral industry, 41-76
  capital expenditures by
  foreign affiliates of U.S.,
  24, 26
  capital expenditures of, in
  LDCs, 31-33, *32*
  expenditures by, for pollution control, *18, 20*
  foreign investments by, 30-31
  future policy for, 139
  as high-pollution industry,
  17
  imports by, 25-28
  imports to U.S. of, goods
  from LDCs, *34*
  investment in foreign, by
  U.S. companies, *23*
  nationalized, in LDCs, 41
  U.S. imports of, goods, *27,
  28*
  see also Metal processors;
  Nonmetallic-mineral
  processors
Minerals
  and arsenic trioxide as by-
  product of, 59-63, *61*
  asbestos, 63-70, *68, 69*
  cement, 63, *72*
  clays, 63
  copper, 44-51, *34*
  exports of processed, by
  foreign affiliates of U.S.
  companies, *29, 30*
  gypsum, 63
  imports to U.S. of processed,
  27, 28, 34

lead, 55-59, *57*
phosphate, 63
potash, 63
silver, *68*
sulfur, 63
zinc, 51-55, *52*
  see also Pollutants
Ministry of National
  Patrimony and Industrial
  Development, Mexico, 67
Montana, 62
Muth, R. J., 48

Namibia, 62n
Naphthalene, 98
National Institute for Occupa-
  tional Safety and Health
  (NIOSH), 96, 114
Netherlands, the, 109
New Jersey, 92
New Jersey Zinc, 53
New York University, 4
Nitric acid, 83
NL Industries, 92-94
Nonenvironmental capital ex-
  penditures. See
  Investments
Nonmetallic-mineral processors
  of cement, 70-75
  effect of environmental and
  workplace standards on,
  63-76
  see also Metal processors
Norway, 44, 93

Obey, David R. (D-Wis.), 5
Obsolescence. See Research
  and development
Occupational Safety and
  Health Administration, 7,
  48, 56, 58, 62, 64, 96,
  109, 114, 121-122

Occupational safety regulations. *See* Environmental regulations
o-Diamisidine, 113
OECD. *See* Organization for Economic Cooperation and Development
Organic chemical processors
of benzidine-based dye products, 113-117
of carbon black, 103-105
effects of environmental and safety regulations on, 95-97
of furfural, 99-103
industry trends, 94-97
of pesticides, 117-123
Organic chemicals, 94-123
benzene, 98
in benzidine-based dyes, 112-117
dynamic demand for, 94-95
environmental problems caused by, 95-97
ethylene, 98
finished products of, 112-123
human health effects of, 96
intermediate, 105-112, *111*. *See also* Benzenoids
methanol, 98
need for data on, 96-97
in pesticides, 117-123
pollution caused by, 96
primary, 97-105
propylene, 98
toluene, 98
world trade in, 95
xylenes, 98
see also Intermediate organic chemicals; Primary organic chemicals
Organization for Economic Cooperation and Development, 28, 30, 75
Organochlorines, 118

Organophosphate-based pesticides, 118
OSHA. *See* Occupational Safety and Health Administration
o-Tolidine, 113
Overseas industrial relocation. *See* Location patterns, international
Overseas Private Investment Corporation, 138

Paraquat, 120
Pennsylvania, 53, 54
Peru, 60, 62
Pesticide producers
effects of environmental and safety regulations on, 5, 117-123
industry trends for, 117-123
location shifts of, 121-122
and product evolution, 118
Pesticides
bentazon, 120
benzenoids, 118-120
chlordimeform, 120
chlorinated, 118
DBCP, 122-123
DDT, 123
dicofol, 123
diuron, 120-121
EDB, 122
exports of, by U.S., 117-118, 117n
imports of benzenoid, by U.S., *119*
imports of, by U.S., 118-121
lindane, 121-122
linuron, 121
organochlorines, 118
organophosphate-based, 118
paraquat, 120
synthetic pyrethroids, 120-121

Treflan, 121
2,4,5-T, 121
2,4,5-TCP, 121
see also Benzenoids;
  Pollutants
Petroleum industry
  expenditures by, for pollu-
    tion control, 18, 20
  see also Organic chemical
    processors
Phelps Dodge, 48
Phenol, 107
Philippines, 60, 63, 99
Phosphates, 63, 86
Phosphoric acid, 83
Phthalic anhydride, 107
Plant siting. See Location pat-
    terns, international
Poland, 99, 115
Policy
  to counter industrial reloca-
    tion, 137-140
  for future environmental
    regulation, 131-140
  for future workplace regula-
    tion, 131-140
  integrative approach to, 140
  to promote reindustrializa-
    tion, 4, 137-140
  need for data for developing,
    9-10
Pollutants
  airborne, 50-51, 63-64
  arsenic trioxide, 59-63, 61
  asbestos, 53, 68, 69
  benzenoid, 111
  butadiene, 108
  carbon black, 106
  from cement manufacture,
    71
  direct dyes, 116
  dust, 71
  furfural, 101
  hydrofluoric acid, 88

from lead processing, 58-59
from inorganic chemical
  processing, 84
naphthalene, 98
sources of, in nonmetallic-
  mineral processing, 63
sulfur dioxide, 45, 50
thiourea, 107, 110
titanium dioxide, 91
xylenes, 98
see also individual
  substances
Pollution-control costs. See
  Expenditures
Pollution-control regulations.
  See Environmental
  regulations
Polyvinyl chloride, 132-133
Potash, 63
Potassium, 86
PPG Industries, 92
Primary organic chemicals
  carbon black, 103-105, 106
  demand for, 97-98
  furfural, 99-103, 101
Production
  of arsenic trioxide, 60-63, 61
  of benzenoids, 109-112
  of benzidine-based dyes,
    114-115, 116
  of carbon black, 103-105,
    106
  of cement, 73
  of copper, 45
  costs of, for metal proces-
    sors, 43-44
  of furfural, 100-103, 101
  by high-growth industries,
    132-133
  of hydrofluoric acid, 86-90,
    88
  of intermediate organic
    chemicals, 107-109
  of lead, 58-59, 57

of primary organic chemicals, 97-98
of titanium, dioxide, 90-93, *91*
of zinc, 51-53, *52*
Production costs. *See* Expenditures; Investments
Propylene, 98
Public opinion
effect of, on polyvinyl chloride production, 132
about titanium dioxide pollution, 94
and U.S. asbestos production, 67
Pulp and paper industry
capital expenditures by foreign affiliates of U.S., *24, 26*
capital expenditures by, in LDCs, *32*
expenditures by, for pollution control, *18, 20*
imports of, goods, *27, 28*
imports to U.S. of, goods from LDCs, *34*

Quaker Oats, 100-103
Quarles, John, 4, 15

Raybestos Manhattan, 67n, 136
Reagan administration, 2, 8, 9
Reagan, Ronald, 8, 9, 15
Regulatory relief. *See* Environmental regulations, relaxing of
Research and development
for cement industry, 71-75
and competitiveness in organic chemical industry, 97
and copper industry, 50-51
importance of, for reindustrialization, 134-136
in inorganic chemical industry, 84
for lead industry, 58-59
in pesticide industry, 118-122
versus regulatory relief, 138-139, 140
in titanium dioxide industry, 93-94
for zinc industry, 51-55
Reverberatory furnace, 50
Romania, 115
Rosenlew process, 99
Runaway shops. *See* Industrial-flight hypothesis

Safety standards. *See* Environmental regulations; Occupational Safety and Health Administration
St. Joe Zinc, 53
Scanlon, Matthew P., 48
SCM Corporation, 90
Sectors, industry. *See* Chemical industry; Mineral industry; Petroleum industry; Pulp and paper industry
Silver, 59
Siting. *See* Location patterns, international
Sodium compounds, 86
South Africa, 89, 99
South America, 48, 122
South Korea, 95
Soviet Union. *See* USSR
Spain, 44, 99
Steel industry, U.S., 42
Strauss, Robert, 8
Styrene monomer, 107
Sulfur, 63
Sulfur dioxide, 45, 50-51

Sulfuric acid, 83, 86, 89
Sweden, 44, 60, 63, 114
Switzerland, 114, 120

Taiwan, 66, *68*
Task Force on Regulatory
    Relief, 9, 15
Tax laws, U.S., 41
Technological innovation. *See*
    Research and development
Terephthalic acid, 107
Tetraethyl lead, 58
Texas, 104
Thiourea, 107-109, 134, *110*
Third World. *See* LDCs
Titanium dioxide, 83, 136
    demand for, 90
    imports of, by U.S., 90-93,
      91
    production of, 90, *91*
    production process for, 93-94
    uses of, 90
Tokyo Round Talks, 8, 47
Toluene, 98
Trade. *See* Exports; Imports
Transportation costs. *See* In-
    vestments; Production
Treasury Department. *See*
    Department of the
    Treasury, U.S.
Treflan, 121
Trinidad, 103
Tsumeb Corporation, 62
2,4-D, 118
2,4,5-T, 121
2,4,5-TCP, 121

United Kingdom, 66, 92, 114,
    68
United Nations Industrial
    Development Organiza-
    tion, 43

United States, 1, 2, 4, 5, 6, 7,
    8, 9, 10, 16, 21, 22,
    25-29, 33, 35, 36, 41, 42,
    43, 44, 44-51, 56, 58-63,
    65-67, 67n, 70-75, 76,
    83-86, 87, 89-90, 90-93,
    94-95, 97, 98-99, 99-103,
    104-105, 107, 109, 112,
    114-115, 117, 117n,
    118-120, 121, 122, 123,
    131-133, 134, 134-136,
    137-140
Uranium, 86
U.S. Industrial Outlook, 112
USSR, 48, 56

Vertical retort furnace, 53-55
Vinyl chloride, 105
Virginia, 92

Wagoner, Joseph, 7
Walter, Ingo, 3, 4, 6, 17
Washington, 60, 62-63
Weidenbaum, Murray L., 8
White arsenic. *See* Arsenic
    trioxide
Workplace health and safety
    regulations. *See* Environ-
    mental regulations; Occu-
    pational Safety and
    Health Administration
World Bank, 75

Xylenes, 98

Zaire, 48
Zambia, 49
Zinc
    and arsenic trioxide by-
      product, 59

effect of environmental and
  safety regulations on,
  smelting, 5
future of U.S., industry, 55,
  77
imports of, 52
industry trends, 51
and LDCs, 54-55
and national security, 55
production process of, 53-54
production of, in U.S., 52
Zinc and Lead International
    Service, 54
Zinc Institute, 54
Zinc oxide, 83

About the Author

H. Jeffrey Leonard, a Conservation Foundation Senior Associate, is responsible for the Foundation's work in Mexico and other Latin American countries. He is the author of *Managing Oregon's Growth: The Politics of Development Planning* and the forthcoming *Pollution and Multinational Corporations in Rapidly Industrializing Nations*, as well as editor of *Divesting Nature's Capital: The Political Economy of Environmental Abuse in the Third World*. Dr. Leonard received his Ph.D. in politics from Princeton University and holds degrees in government and economics from the London School of Economics.